WOMEN AND THE NEWS

WOMEN
AND
THE NEWS

Edited, and with an Introduction

by

LAURILY KEIR EPSTEIN

COMMUNICATION ARTS BOOKS

HASTINGS HOUSE, PUBLISHERS
New York 10016

Library of Congress Cataloging in Publication data

Main entry under title:

Women and the news.

    (Communication art books)
    The result of a conference held at Washington University,
St. Louis, in Sept. 1977, and sponsored by Washington Univer-
sity and the Monticello College Foundation.
    Includes bibliographical references and index.
    I. Women in the press—United States. 2. Women
in journalism—United States. I. Epstein, Laurily Keir.
II. Washington University, St. Louis. III. Monticello College
Foundation.
PN4888.W65W6   070.4'8347'0973   78-16556

ISBN 0-8038-8087-1

Published simultaneously in Canada by
Copp Clark Ltd., Toronto
Printed in the United States of America

Contents

List of Tables

Introduction

THIS VOLUME is the result of a two-day conference on women and the news held at Washington University (St. Louis) in September, 1977. The conference was based on the general, and presumably unarguable, premise that there is a relationship between what is reported as news and what individuals and groups think of as socially and politically important. Although this premise may be unassailable, the theoretical and empirical ramifications of the relationship have only recently been subjected to systematic investigation. Recent findings in the field make it clear that the media play an important role in defining women's status. Thus, for those to whom improving the status of women is a matter of concern, understanding the relationship of the press to society in general, and to women more specifically, is justifiably important.

The conference was designed to examine three current concepts of particular interest in news media research: agenda-setting, access to the media, and definitions of the news. A brief look at each concept should help clarify it, the type of research it generates and its relevance to women's concerns.

AGENDA-SETTING

Those who study the news media as agenda-setters assume that audiences take note of what is emphasized in the news and then incorporate these emphases into their personal agendas, i.e., into their personal list of meaningful or salient political issues.[1] Although this potential for agenda-setting was realized some time ago by observers as diverse as Walter Lippmann[2] and political sociologists Paul Lazarsfeld, Bernard Berelson and Hazel Gaudet,[3] impetus for systematic research in agenda-setting began with Bernard Cohen's study of the press and foreign policy in 1963.[4] In that study, Cohen asserted, "[the press] may not be successful much of the time in telling people what to think, but it is stunningly successful in telling its readers what to think *about*."[5]

Since Cohen's study, various researchers have begun investigating how, to what extent and under what conditions the mass media set the agenda for their audiences. Most of these studies have examined the coverage of presidential elections and individual voter's perceptions of salient political issues.[6] More recently, however, elections below the presidential level have been examined;[7] in addition, press treatment of non-electoral political issues is coming under serious scrutiny.[8] One of the more intriguing findings of these studies is that newspapers, not television, are the agenda-setters.[9]

There are, then, two important assumptions inherent in the agenda-setting concept. The first is that what is emphasized in the news becomes translated into what is important either to the individuals reading the news or to the society absorbing the news. The second is that it is newspapers, not television, which set our agendas.

If these assumptions about agenda-setting are tenable, then women's issues will not be accorded high priority in our society until newspapers cover them as thoroughly and as prominently as other issues. We need not engage in large-scale content analyses to learn that, even today, women and women's issues are treated idiosyncratically when they are treated at all. The media may have moved away from describing a leading nuclear physicist as "a petite grandmother of five," but the press still does not cover women in a fashion that would lead individuals to understand the myriad dramatic changes in women's lives in our society. If women are to succeed and to be taken seriously in academic or professional life and if the press is one of the factors giving credibility to groups and issues in our society, it is essential that we understand better how and under what conditions the press helps to set our societal agenda and what this means to and for women.

Chapter I of this volume, by Maxwell McCombs, presents an overview of the theoretical aspects of agenda-setting. Chapter II, by Doris A. Graber, applies the agenda-setting concept to women and women's issues; her data are drawn from 1,500 interviews conducted throughout the 1976 calendar year. Chapters I and II are written by academic researchers and as such, reflect either theoretical or systematic empirical viewpoints. They stand in contrast to Chapter III, written by Patricia Rice, a feature writer for the *St. Louis Post-Dispatch,* who presents an insider's view of the news media. The differences between the McCombs and Graber chapters and the Rice chapter are, perhaps, the differences between the pristine groves of academe and the real world or, if you will, the differences between the entomologist and the beetle.

Access to the Media

Access to the media as a field for research began with Jerome Barron's seminal article, "Access to the News—A New First Amendment Right."[10] In that article, expanded later into a book,[11] Barron argues that denial of access by the media constitutes an abridgment of First Amendment rights to disadvantaged groups. Noting that blacks, women, the poor, unpopular political groups and other marginal groups are often denied access to the media, Barron maintains that a latter-twentieth century interpretation of freedom of the press mandates full access to the media for all.[12]

A recent empirical study of access to the media by Edie Goldenberg examined the news treatment of four resource-poor groups in Boston.[13] She concludes that the organization within and the structure of newspapers interact with marginal groups' lack of visibility to produce little, if any, coverage of such groups and the issues important to them.

The assumption underlying access to the media is that disadvantaged groups are denied the same type of coverage as well-defined and well-accepted non-marginal groups. Those espousing access assume that, if freedom of speech is more than mere rhetoric, society must provide access to the press for those who are unlikely to receive coverage for reasons other than "non-newsworthiness." For women, a traditionally marginal group economically and politically, the question is how to gain more equitable access to the press. Today, women who adhere to extremist positions make news; moderate academic and professional women typically do not. Why? What, if anything, can be done so that women's access to the press is increased?

Tentative answers to these questions are found in Chapters IV through VI. Chapter IV, by Edie Goldenberg, presents a general view of the access to the media argument. MaryAnn Yodelis Smith, in Chapter V, sets forth the legal and constitutional problems encountered by women and minorities as they attempt to insure fair treatment by and access to the media without encroaching on or eroding the First Amendment rights of other social groups. In Chapter VI,

Gertrude Joch Robinson discusses the symbolic processes of group legitimation by the media. Previous studies and current data from both the United States and Canada are used by Professor Robinson.

DEFINITIONS OF THE NEWS

Definitions of the news range from the descriptive to the banal. · For example, a former editor of the *New York Times* stated, "My own definition of news is that it is something you didn't know before, had forgotten or didn't understand."[14] Although reporters usually offer definitions equally opaque of what is news, researchers in this area are beginning to find evidence that the organizational and structural considerations of the news media are more likely to define what is newsworthy than are the "objective realities" of what actually happens in the world on any given day.[15]

Edward Jay Epstein's study of television news, *News From Nowhere*,[16] emphasizes that structural demands "create" the evening news we see on television. For example, the quality of the picture is far more important to a television news story than is the actual content of the story. Moreover, the time it takes to film a story, develop the film and edit it makes east coast morning events more frequent "news" than west coast late afternoon events.

Leon Sigal's study of the front page makeup of the *New York Times* and the *Washington Post* emphasizes the organizational perspective of news making.[17] He stresses that the news is a result of the routines reporters follow for collecting information—e.g., the beat system, source placement and credibility, official releases—and of the division of labor within news organizations—e.g., conflicts between reporters and editors, bureaus, reporters on different beats, different types of editors.

Less systematic but nonetheless profound studies of the press and the political system are Timothy Crouse's *The Boys on the Bus*[18] and the "Woodstein" book, *All the President's Men*.[19] Crouse's treatment of press coverage of the 1972 presidential campaign emphasizes, among other things, the fact that a story must be carried on either the AP or UPI wires or in the *New York Times* or the *Washington Post* before other papers will cover the story. That is, an important event may happen, but if one of those four news sources does not carry the story, no other editor will accept it as news. In *All the President's Men*, the authors discuss the problems they encountered with continuing their story once it had gone from a local petty crime story (metropolitan desk) to a major news event (national desk). What becomes clear is that the symbiotic relationship of the White House reporters and the White House press office precluded those reporters' realization that the June, 1972, break-in was "news."[20]

Since definitions of news or newsworthiness appear to be predicated partially on organizational or structural considerations, it is important to understand the interaction of these considerations with "objective reality." If the beat system, source placement and credibility shape the news and if editors are anticipating audience reaction to the news, how does this affect women and women's issues and what structural changes might conduce to more equitable coverage of women and women's issues?

Chapter VII, by Leon Sigal, is an overview of the viewpoint that the structure and organization of the news media shape and define the news. Chapter VIII, written by Suzanne Pingree and Robert Hawkins, looks at the effects definitions of the news have on women and women's issues.

Grateful acknowledgment must be made to the sponsors of the conference, the Monticello College Foundation and Washington University. The conference was part of the Mr. and Mrs. Spencer T. Olin Fellowship Program for Women, named for two leading benefactors of the Monticello College Foundation. This program provides four years of fellowship support for women seeking a Ph.D. or a terminal degree in higher education and the professions at Washington University. Students are chosen on the basis of a nationwide competition and matriculate at Washington University. In addition to the fellowships, the Monticello College Foundation provides for an annual conference devoted to women and the special problems they confront in academic and professional life.

Special thanks for almost everything are given to Kathryn A. Baer, Assistant Professor of English and Director of Women's Studies, Washington University; Ralph Morrow, Dean of the Graduate School of Arts and Sciences, Washington University; and JoHanna Potts, of the Student Affairs Office of Washington University.

L.K.E.

NOTES

[1] A useful definition of agenda-building is found in *Participation in American Politics: The Dynamics of Agenda-Building,* Roger W. Cobb and Charles D. Elder (Boston: Allyn and Bacon, Inc., 1972).

[2] *Public Opinion* (New York: The Free Press, 1965, originally 1922).

[3] *The People's Choice* (New York: Columbia University Press, 1948).

[4] *The Press and Foreign Policy* (Princeton: Princeton University Press, 1963).

[5] *Ibid.*, p. 13.

[6] Most of this work has been done by Maxwell McCombs and his associates. See, for example, Maxwell McCombs and Donald Shaw, "The Agenda-Setting Function of the Media," *Public Opinion Quarterly*, 36 (1972), pp. 176–87.

[7] L. P. Tipton, R. D. Haney and J. R. Basehart, "Media Agenda-Setting in City and State Campaigns," *Journalism Quarterly*, 52 (1975), pp. 15–22.

[8] G. R. Funkhouser, "The Issues of the Sixties: An Exploratory Study in the Dynamics of Public Opinion," *Public Opinion Quarterly*, 37 (1973), pp. 62–75; ——, "Trends in Media Coverage of the Issues of the Sixties," *Journalism Quarterly*, 50 (1973), pp. 535–38; W. T. Gormley, "Newspaper Agendas and Political Elites," *Journalism Quarterly*, 52 (1975), pp. 304–8.

[9] This viewpoint is expounded at length in a recent study in which the authors found that voters learn more hard information from paid political advertising than from the evening network news. Thomas E. Patterson and Robert D. McClure, *The Unseeing Eye* (New York: G. P. Putnam's Sons, 1976).

[10] *Harvard Law Review*, 80 (1967).

[11] *Freedom of the Press for Whom? The Right of Access to Mass Media* (Bloomington: Indiana University Press, 1975).

[12] Given the ambiguities of what free access to all means and how it would be accomplished, it is not surprising that Barron's argument has generated spirited debate among lawyers and publishers. A recent rebuttal to Barron is found in Benno C. Schmidt, Jr., *Freedom of the Press vs. Public Access* (New York: Praeger, 1976).

[13] *Making the Papers* (Lexington, Massachusetts: Lexington Books, 1975).

[14] Attributed to Turner Catledge.

[15] A recent sociological study of news definitions is Bernard Roshco's *Newsmaking* (Chicago: University of Chicago Press, 1975).

[16] New York: Vintage Books, 1974.

[17] *Reporters and Officials* (Lexington, Massachusetts: Lexington Books, 1973).

[18] New York: Ballantine Books, 1973.

[19] Carl Bernstein and Robert Woodward (New York: Simon and Schuster, 1974).

[20] The work of Richard Hofstetter and his colleagues on the Television Election News Coverage Project (1972) investigates yet another aspect of news and its definitions: how to ascertain bias and objectivity. In a voluminous series of working papers, Hofstetter *et. al.* examine both the theoretical and empirical aspects of defining both bias and objectivity. The question of bias in the news was addressed most loudly by Spiro Agnew in his famous Des Moines, Iowa, speech in 1969. His assertions on bias in the news gave rise to numerous studies on objectivity and bias in the news; the net result of these studies is that the news is far less biased than Agnew said it was. The most important and publicized exception to these findings is Edith Efron, *The News Twisters* (Los Angeles: Nash Publishing, 1971).

I

Public Response
to the Daily News

by **MAXWELL E. McCOMBS**
Syracuse University

DAILY SURVEILLANCE of the world out there, whether by news organizations or by individual interested citizens, requires a great many decisions about what to scan. Out of the many competing events, topics and situations, which ones should be selected for attention?

Fortunately for reporters and editors, the traditional news values of journalism provide general guidance about what to select and what to ignore. Some persons, events and situations clearly are more *newsworthy* than others! For individual citizens, the solution to this dilemma of where to direct one's attention is less explicit, but nevertheless present.

An increasing volume of behavioral science research documents that individual—and community—perceptions of what are the important concerns of the day are influenced by the news media's daily portrayals of the world. Accumulating empirical evidence suggests that

1

editors and news directors through their day-by-day selection and display of the news provide their audiences with major cues about the relative importance of issues and other topics in the news. In other words, press coverage influences the *perceived salience* of topics—especially social issues—in the audience's mind. While the communication of these saliences is an inevitable by-product of journalists' daily necessity to select a few news items for attention, these cues are among the most important elements communicated by the news media. It is this ability of the press to significantly structure our perceptions of the world, particularly our perceptions of which social issues are most important, that has come to be called the *agenda-setting function of the press*.[1] It is the press which sets the agenda for public attention and public discussion.

In a very basic sense, this influence of the press is a truism! To a considerable degree, the public reacts only to those things of which the press makes them aware. Most of the relevant world of social issues and significant action on those issues is out of sight and not experienced firsthand by the average citizen. But the agenda-setting influence of the press is more pervasive and detailed than simple awareness. This influence of the press on the perceived salience of social issues is such that over time the priorities of the press become to a considerable degree the priorities of the public.

Now it is important to distinguish this cognitive influence of the press described by the metaphor of agenda-setting from any influence of the press on attitudes and opinions. Most considerations of public opinion concentrate on attitudes and opinions, people's affective feelings of liking or disliking, of being for or against something. Four decades of empirical research clearly demonstrates the limited impact of mass communication on the attitudes and opinions of its audience.

This distinction between attitudes and cognitions, and the impact of mass media on each, is succinctly summed up in Bernard Cohen's remark[2] that while the mass media may not tell us what to think, they definitely tell us what to think *about*.

The evidence is increasingly clear that the press does play a major role in telling us what to think about. Furthermore, the press itself plays this role in focusing our attention quite independent of its news sources and the events and situations of the real world. This is not to say that the press creates news from whole cloth. It does not! But so much is happening in the world each day that the press must select. And because there is so much to select from, there is considerable latitude in the application of traditional news values.

THE PRESS, PUBLIC OPINION AND REALITY

In a review of public opinion trends across the entire decade of the 1960s, public opinion researcher G. Ray Funkhouser[3] juxtaposed three elements:

- the agenda of the press, exemplified in its pattern of coverage for the decade;
- the public agenda, inferred from national public opinion polls asking people what they regarded as the major issues of the day;
- statistical indicators of trends in the real world, for example, the number of troops committed to Vietnam as a measure of actual U.S. concern and commitment on that issue.

Comparison of press coverage with public perceptions of what were the most important issues yielded a substantial correlation (+.78). Table 1–1 shows that for only a single topic—mass media coverage of itself—did the discrepancy between the rankings on the press

TABLE 1-1

Coverage in National News Magazines and Rankings of "Most Important Problem Facing America" During 1960s

Issue	Number of Articles	Coverage Rank	Importance Rank
Vietnam war	861	1	1
Race relations (and urban riots)	687	2	2
Campus unrest	267	3	4
Inflation	234	4	5
Television and mass media	218	5	12*
Crime	203	6	3
Drugs	173	7	9
Environment and pollution	109	8	6
Smoking	99	9	12*
Poverty	74	10	7
Sex (declining morality)	62	11	8
Women's rights	47	12	12*
Science and society	37	13	12*
Population	36	14	12*

*These items were never noted as "the most important problem" in the Gallup findings, so are ranked equally below the items that did.

(Funkhouser, 1973)

Reprinted with permission of *Public Opinion Quarterly*.

and public agendas exceed more than three. It is perhaps not surprising that while the mass media pay a great deal of attention to themselves, this attention is not translated into public concern.

Now, of course, every issue listed in Table 1–1 was not cited every year in the public opinion polls as one of the most important issues facing the country. But an additional comparison of whether an issue was cited with whether the press coverage was heavy or light that year (based on the average for the decade) again shows a strong correlation between press coverage and public perceptions of an issue's importance. As Funkhouser notes, there were only nine exceptions, instances where the level of press coverage and mentions in public opinion polls did not match. Three of these concerned inflation, which seems unlikely to depend on press coverage for public notice. A fourth was a peak in early press coverage of drugs and the "flower children," which preceded any public recognition of drugs as a major social issue.

Further analysis of the press coverage during the 1960s reveals the lack of any one-to-one relationship with the actualities of any of the issues. Press coverage of—as well as public concern over—the Vietnam war, campus unrest and urban riots peaked a year or so before the actual situations reached their zenith. Press coverage of two issues, drugs and inflation, did closely parallel the actualities of the real world. But press coverage of race relations, crime, poverty and pollution showed little correlation with the actualities of the real world, nor did the coverage of the five remaining issues listed in Table 1–1, issues which were never cited as "most important" in the public opinion polls. This last group of issues represents a dual set of discrepancies: press coverage of these issues matched neither the actualities of the real world nor the trends in public opinion. However, this latter discrepancy between press coverage and public concern may be more apparent than real. Note that three of these issues missing from the public agenda fall at the bottom of the press agenda.

To sum up, a comparison of the historical trends across the 1960s found a substantial correlation between press coverage and public concern. This is in line with the idea of an agenda-setting function of the press. This assertion of a major press influence on public opinion is further strengthened by the general absence of any correlation between the actualities of the real world and either press coverage or public concern about these major social issues.

While the press is the major conduit between the public and most of the issues on which public opinion focuses, it is a conduit with a considerable number of gatekeepers. These gatekeepers include the reporter who writes the original version and numerous editors who handle and modify it along the way. The news messages transmitted by these gatekeepers reflect journalistic news values and perceptions of audience needs and interests as well as what is happening in the real world. It is not surprising that little correlation exists between the press agenda and the actualities of the real world.

To mix metaphors, the light from the mirror to the world held up by the daily press is refracted through a number of prisms before that picture is viewed by the general public. Even more clearly than the original image on the mirror, this refracted and simplified image of reality in the daily news contains major cues about the relative importance of various issues and events. Newspapers clearly communicate the salience of a topic through page placement, headline size and the amount of space. Television news formats also provide cues about the relative salience of news events.

The idea of an agenda-setting function of mass communication is an assertion that audiences learn these saliences from the mass media and incorporate a similar set of weights into their own personal agendas. Agenda-setting specifies a positive relationship between the emphases of the news media and the perceived importance of these topics to the news audience. In short, the press agenda largely determines the public agenda.

Understanding Agenda-Setting and Public Opinion

To fully understand the role of the agenda-setting function of the press in the formation of public opinion, it is necessary to examine several facets of this idea in detail. Here we will examine three facets of the core *concept* of agenda-setting, plus one facet of the larger *theory* of agenda-setting which is growing out of this conceptual development.

To understand the basic concept of agenda-setting and its role in public opinion we need to consider in detail:

- the nature of the public agenda;
- the nature of the mass media agendas;
- the time lag between the appearance of items on the press agenda and their later appearance on the public agenda.

Public Agendas.

In considering the public agenda—those issues or topics in the forefront of public attention and concern—it is important to make several distinctions. First, for each individual we must distinguish between the *intrapersonal agenda*—those things that are personally most important to the individual—and the *interpersonal agenda*—those things that the individual discusses most often with others.

While there is considerable overlap between the contents of these two agendas, it is far from perfect.[4] Many topics of major concern to an individual may never show up as prominent topics of discussion with friends or family. Conversely, a great deal of the content of daily conversation focuses on the trivial and topics of passing moment, not the abiding issues and concerns of the time.

As we see in Table 1–2, taken from a study of public opinion

TABLE 1-2

Issue "Talked About Most Frequently" by Issue "Considered Personally Most Important"

		TALKED ABOUT MOST FREQUENTLY				
		Rising Prices	Middle East	Watergate	Energy/ Environment	Other
A.	Rising Prices (n = 32)	15.6%	21.9%	62.5%			100%
B.	Middle East (n = 51)		49.0%	51.0%			100%
C.	Watergate (n = 116)	2.6%	12.1%	82.8%	1.7%	0.9%	100%
D.	Energy Environment (n = 26)		15.4%	73.1%	11.5%		100%
E.	Other (n = 35)	2.9%	8.6%	51.4%		37.1%	100%

(Row label at left: PERSONALLY MOST IMPORTANT)

x^2 = 141.88, 16dF, p < .001

Contingency Coefficient = 0.59

(McCombs, 1974)

among college students in 1973, only for a single issue—Watergate—did a majority of the students name the same issue as the one they talked about the most *and* considered personally most important. If there were perfect agreement between the interpersonal and intrapersonal agendas, all the entries in Table 1–2 would fall along the principal diagonal. As it turns out, just over half (54.6%) of the entries fall along the diagonal. The others are quite scattered.

In this specific set of public opinion data, Watergate is the principal reason for the scatter and the discrepancy between the two agendas. While a majority of students reported talking more about Watergate than any other issue, less than half (44.6%) designated Watergate as their most important personal concern. But there is a scatter for all the other issues in Table 1–2 also.

Beyond these two types of personal agendas, each individual also perceives a community agenda—those things which he or she believes to be the major concerns of the community in which he or she reside.[5] Our experience during the 1976 elections illustrates the divergence between personal agendas and perceived community agendas. Among our random sample of respondents interviewed in New Hampshire, for example, few persons listed taxes as a major personal concern, although the vast majority told us that taxes were the major concern of most voters in their community.

So in our consideration of the focus of public opinion, and the influence of the press on the focus, we need to distinguish three different agendas:

- the intrapersonal agenda;
- the interpersonal agenda;
- the perceived community agenda.

In the tradition of public opinion polling, most of the empirical research to date has focused on the intrapersonal agenda, those things about which each individual is personally concerned. But each of these public agendas represents a significant focus.

Media Agendas.

While most scholars have used quite straightforward content analysis procedures to study the agendas of the mass media, there is always the question of which mass media to include. Most studies have used a mix of media, the favorites being television and newspapers because they are the dominant mass communication channels for news.

At first, television and newspapers were used in tandem as simply two major news outlets. But recent work has begun to outline distinct and separate agenda-setting roles for television and newspapers. In other words, television and newspaper influence are not simple replicates of each other.

For example, a recent book, *The Emergence of American Political Issues*,[6] reports data indicating a major agenda-setting role on political issues for newspapers and only a minor role for TV. The gist of that evidence is this: Newspapers are the prime movers in organizing the public agenda. Exerting a cumulative influence that extends across many weeks, they largely set the stage of public concern. But television news is not wholly without influence. It does have some short-term impact on the composition of the public agenda.

Using data collected in Charlotte, North Carolina, during the 1972 Presidential election, the book documents a significant relationship between newspaper coverage in June and the public agenda of voters during October. No comparable influence was found for television news, so the initial long-term influence in defining the fall agenda of political issues seems clearly to be with newspapers. But when we examine the short-term influences of each medium, the picture is reversed. The strong impact of newspapers reflected in the June-to-October relationship disappears. But the short-term strength of the relationship between the television agenda and the public agenda is considerable. While television is not restructuring the total agenda, it clearly influences the rank-ordering of issues at the top of the agenda.

Perhaps the best way to describe and contrast these influences is to label the role of the newspaper as long-term *agenda-setting* and the role of television as short-term *spotlighting*. The basic nature of the agenda seems often to be set by the newspapers, while television primariy reorders or rearranges the top items on the agenda. The medium may not be the message, but the medium affects the impact of the message.

Time Lag.

This description of the separate and distinct roles played by newspapers and television raises the question of what is the time lag between the appearance of an item on the press agenda and the appearance of that item on the public agenda. Our best evidence to date suggests that a three- to five-month process, on the average, is involved in the agenda-setting influence of the print media.[7]

As we see in Figure 1-1, the degree of correlation between the

FIGURE 1-1

Correlations of the Public Agenda With Various Press Agendas

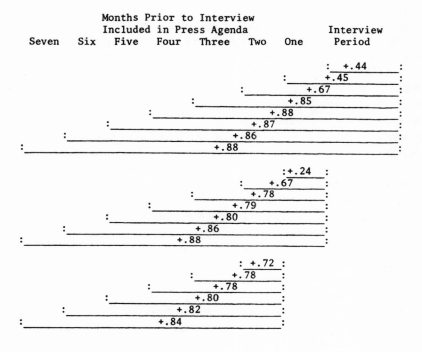

(Stone, 1975)

press agenda and the public agenda of college students—the same students described in Table 1–2—steadily increases as the press agenda is expanded to include the accumulation of material from more and more weeks.[8] When the public agenda is compared with the press agenda from the same month in which the public opinion survey was conducted or that month plus the previous month, the correlations are quite modest (.44 and .45). But as more months of material are added to the press agenda, the correlations increase. A press agenda defined in terms of press coverage during the month of the interviews plus the four previous months yields the strongest correlation (.88). This pattern at the top of Figure 1–1 is clearly in line with the assertion just made that agenda-setting is a three- to five-month process.

This time frame continues to hold when the press coverage during the interview month or even the month before the interviews is omitted from consideration. Looking at the other two parts of Figure 1–1, we see that the correlation coefficients reach their zenith when the press agenda is based on material three to five months prior to the survey used to establish the public agenda.

That, of course, is an average based on a total agenda containing many items. A few issues move almost instantaneously from the press to the public agenda. Others, like Watergate, take a long period of incubation before they appear on the public agenda in any strength. As we saw in the detailed analysis of the 1972 Presidential election, voter concerns of the early fall largely reflected press coverage of the late spring and early summer. One of our continuing concerns in this research is to identify the variations in this learning process among news audiences, variations among types of issues and among different kinds of individuals.

This question of the time lag in the movement of topics from the press agenda to the public agenda does help answer an additional question about the nature of the press agenda. The concept of agenda-setting is not pertinent to every issue or concern which a society confronts. There are boundaries to agenda-setting, defined in part by journalism's view of the nature of news and in part by the tenure of that news.

First of all, mass communication agendas and, hence, the agenda-setting influence, are limited to that range of topics considered newsworthy. For many topics, the press will play no role at all in bringing them to public consciousness. Second, if the newsworthy aspects of a topic or concern do not persist over time, the press is unlikely to play any significant agenda-setting role. The three- to five-month average lag in time just described reflects a continuing, long-term influence process, one of slow accretion rather than rapid "Ah ha!" effects. If a topic does not stay in the news over a considerable period of time, there is likely to be little impact on the public agenda.

More Than Issues

To this point, we have talked primarily about the influence of the press on the broad public agenda of issues. But the concept of agenda-setting is not limited to the relationship between the salience of issues in the mass media and the salience of those issues to the audience. In addition to providing cues about the relative salience of issues, the mass media also differentiate between the salience of various attributes or facets of each of those issues. Not every attribute of an issue, idea or event in the news is considered newsworthy. Among those attributes selected for mention in the news, all are not accorded equal treatment. Just as the issues in the news have different saliences, the attributes of those issues also have different saliences!

Two recent studies have demonstrated that the influence of the mass media on the perceived salience of attributes of issues in the news is equal to its influence in placing the issues themselves on the public agenda. This adds a new theoretical dimension to the assertion that the mass media structure our perceptions of the world.

TABLE 1-3

Correlations of Media Coverage of Economic Proposals with Respondent's Agenda

Newspaper Agenda With Newspaper Reader's Agenda	Newspaper Agenda With TV Viewer's Agenda	TV Agenda With TV Viewer's Agenda	TV Agenda With Newspaper Reader's Agend
r = +.81	r = +.62	r = +.27	r = +.16
n = 13	n = 13	n = 13	n = 13
p <.01	p <.05	n.s.	n.s.

(Benton and Frazier, 1976)

Reprinted with permission of *Communication Research*.

Focusing on a major contemporary agenda item, the economy, Benton and Frazier studied the relationship between press coverage and public perceptions of Minneapolis residents across three major sets of attributes of this general issue.[9] They examined such specific economic problems as high food prices, inflation and unemployment; specific causes like Arab oil prices and bad weather conditions; and such proposed solutions as gas rationing, and tax rebates. Here probing into the agenda-setting influence of the press within a single major issue, Benton and Frazier again found striking correlations between the salience among the general public of these facets of the economic issue and their coverage in *some* of the mass media.

Table 1–3 shows a substantial correlation between the local newspaper agenda and the agenda of Minneapolis residents reporting major reliance on newspapers for public affairs information. In marked contrast, the correlation is low and non-significant between the television agenda and the agenda of residents relying predominantly upon television for public affairs information. This pattern of findings in Table 1–3 for the agenda-setting roles of newspapers and television news repeats the pattern previously described for the 1972 Charlotte Presidential election study. But the more valuable contribution of the Minneapolis study is its demonstration of agenda-setting effects at a second level, the attributes and facets of an item on the agenda of major public issues.

Similar results were obtained by Cohen, who studied the details of a local public issue, development of a large lake area in Indiana.[10] Again, public perceptions of this issue were compared with the various facets reported in the local press—sewage, roads and traffic, condominiums and commercial development versus recreation and natural preservation. In this study the public agenda was ascertained in three ways: open-ended questions soliciting issues of most interest; issues that had been discussed the most; matched pairs of issues that were ranked by the public. The correlations between press coverage and these three measures of the public agenda were +.60, +.61, and +.71, respectively. In line with our previous comparisons of newspapers and television, it should be noted that the press coverage here is that of the local newspaper only.

Again, there is evidence that the press is effective not only in communicating a broad array or agenda of issues, but also is effective in communicating an array of their attributes as well. In short, there is evidence in hand of the ability of the press, especially newspapers, to influence public perceptions. Both the Minneapolis and Indiana investigations also document this agenda-setting role outside the setting of election campaigns.

Consideration of agenda-setting in terms of the saliences of both general topics and their attributes subsumes several similar ideas encountered in past discussions of mass media influence. The concepts of *status-conferral, image-making* and *stereotyping* all concern the salience of objects and/or their attributes.

Status-conferral describes the ability of the mass media to influence the perceived importance of a person. Image-making, typically used to describe election campaign strategy, covers both efforts to place a candidate's name high on the voters' agenda or roster of viable candidates and efforts to structure the attributes or characteristics of the candidate perceived to be most salient and important. Stereotyping deals with the salience of attributes, the cluster of characteristics prominent in the characterization or perceived image of some group, such as women.

Numerous content analyses in recent years have detailed the stereotypical treatment of women in popular television drama, elementary school readers, daily news reports and other mass media messages. The concept of an agenda-setting influence of the press adds an important complement to these content analyses. For the most part, these content analyses are literally just that—analyses and descriptions of the attributes on the media agenda. They are single variable studies, not comprehensive studies of the relationship between the media agenda and the public response. Research is now beginning to map this relationship, and agenda-setting offers one major perspective for examining this situation, a perspective that raises a number of detailed questions and links this concern to the entire realm of public opinion.

Summing Up

The concept—and emerging theory—of an agenda-setting function of the press offers a detailed perspective on the nature of the influence that mass media have on the issues and images prominent in the public mind. Some of the accumulating empirical evidence that has been presented here describes four key aspects of this influence process:

- Nature of the public agenda: While there is considerable overlap in what people talk about and what they consider personally most important, these are distinct agendas of public concerns.
- Mass media agendas: A variety of empirical evidence suggests that newspapers play a more dominant role than television news in the agenda-setting process.
- Nature of this influence on learning process: While short-term agenda-setting effects have been demonstrated, this seems to be basically a long-term, continuing process requiring several months on the average for items to move from the media agenda to the public agenda.
- Range of effects: While most investigations have focused on a broad array or agenda of public issues, several studies show similar effects on the perception of individual public issues, an agenda of attributes, if you will.

What is emerging from this welter of detail is a comprehensive, theoretical picture of the early, formative stages of public opinion, a picture of public response to the daily news.

NOTES

[1] Maxwell McCombs and Donald Shaw, "The Agenda-Setting Function of Mass Media," *Public Opinion Quarterly*, 36 (1972), pp. 176–87; Lee Becker, Maxwell MccCombs and Jack McLeod, "The Development of Political Cognitions," in Steven Chaffee, ed. *Political Communication* (Beverly Hills: Sage Publications, 1975); Donald Shaw and Maxwell McCombs, *The Emergence of American Political Issues: The Agenda-Setting Function of the Press* (St. Paul: West Publishing Company, 1977).

[2] Bernard Cohen, *The Press and Foreign Policy* (Princeton: Princeton University Press, 1963).

[3] G. Ray Funkhouser, "The Issues of the Sixties: An Exploratory Study in the Dynamics of Public Opinion," *Public Opinion Quarterly*, 37 (1973), pp. 62–75.

[4] Maxwell McCombs, "A Comparison of Intrapersonal and Interpersonal Agendas of Public Issues," International Communication Association (New Orleans, Louisiana, 1974).

[5] Jack McLeod, Lee Becker and J. E. Byrnes, "Another Look at the Agenda-Setting Function of the Press," *Communication Research*, 1 (1974), pp. 131–66; Elisabeth Noelle-Neumann, "Turbulances in the Climate of Opinion: Methodological Applications of the Spiral of Silence Theory," *Public Opinion Quarterly*, 41 (1977), pp. 143–58.

[6] Shaw and McCombs, *The Emergence of American Political Issues, op. cit.*

[7] Gerald Stone, "Tracing the Time Lag in Agenda-Setting," *Studies in Agenda-Setting*, Communication Research Center (Syracuse University, 1975); Shaw and McCombs, *op. cit.*

[8] Stone, *op. cit.*

[9] Marc Benton and P. J. Frazier, "The Agenda-Setting Function of the Mass Media at Three Levels of Information-Holding," *Communication Research*, 3 (1976), pp. 261–74.

[10] D. Cohen, "A Report on a Non-Election Agenda-Setting Study," Association for Education in Journalism (Ottawa, Canada, 1975).

II

Agenda-Setting: Are There Women's Perspectives?

by **DORIS A. GRABER**

University of Illinois at Chicago Circle

INTRODUCTION

CONTEMPORARY FOLK WISDOM has it that women differ from men in political interest and knowledge. Politics is still widely considered as a man's business into which comparatively few women stray. Women as a group are portrayed as political "primitives" who are proud of their aloofness from what is considered to be very dirty business, indeed.[1] Is the stereotype essentially true, in whole or in part? Specifically, is there a difference between men and women in the way they select news items for attention and in their rankings of what is and what is not important in today's world? In short, do "agendas" differ?

These questions will be answered here, using information gathered throughout the 1976 calendar year. The information consists of transcripts and records of some 1,500 interviews conducted at roughly six-week intervals with four small panels of voters. Two of these panels were located in Evanston, Illinois; the other two were in Indianapolis, Indiana, and in Lebanon, New Hampshire. The panel members were selected from a random sample of voters to represent a demographic cross section and various degrees of interest in politics. Care was also taken that the sample contained people with large and small amounts of time available for using the media, and people who relied primarily on newspapers or on television for their news, as well as people who relied equally on both.[2]

The interviews were matched by a year-long content analysis of newspapers and television news in the Chicago, Indianapolis and Lebanon areas. The print media which were content-analyzed on a daily or sample basis were the *Chicago Tribune,* the *Chicago Daily News,* the *Chicago Sun-Times,* the *Indianapolis News,* the *Indianapolis Star* and the *Lebanon Valley News.* For television content, the early evening newscasts on ABC, CBS and NBC national news were analyzed, as well as CBS and NBC local news in the Chicago areas.[3] These media were selected because they were the ones which the panel members used primarily for information.

Three of the panels were composed of 48 respondents; the fourth panel had 21 respondents and was used for intensive analysis to provide in-depth data to supplement the information obtained from the larger panels. The core panel, located in Evanston, was interviewed in depth with lengthy, open-ended taped interviews conducted in the panelists' homes.

Members of the panel also completed daily diaries in which they recorded news stories that had come to their attention. The diaries, filled out after a lapse of time in news exposure, presented brief accounts of news stories as well as comments about the panel members' reactions to the stories and reasons for remembering them over a period of time ranging from a few hours to an entire day or more. Panel members who were unwilling or unable to fill out their own diaries were contacted by an interviewer by telephone who then made diary entries for them.

In addition, core panel members regularly answered questions about specific news stories that had appeared in the media, giving whatever facts they recalled along with reasons for remembering these facts. During the course of the interview year, story recall for roughly 250 stories was recorded for each core panel respondent.

Our research design thus assured that we had a panel evenly divided between men and women, and exposed to similar news stories, whose political learning and agenda formation we had monitored for an entire year. We also had a complete content analysis of their information sources from which we could ascertain the news agendas that had been available to our panelists.

We used these data to answer three questions: (1) Most importantly, we wanted to know in what ways, if any, men's and women's agendas of significant news items differed. Assuming that agenda formation hinges in part on availability of news and the prominence with which it is featured, we also wanted to know (2) whether the media made it feasible to form agendas of "women's topics," if women, like interest groups, wished to focus more heavily on topics that might be of special concern to them. "Women's topics" here refers to issues like family welfare, health, education, rape and child abuse, which are widely believed to be matters of special concern to women.[4] (3) Lastly, we wanted to inquire what background factors and aspects of women's current social setting might possibly explain the patterns of agenda formation among women.

Throughout the analysis, we divided our panels into age as well as sex groups to capture age-linked changes that might be due to life-cycle stages or to different experiences in the formative years.[5] In the tables, the abbreviation OW and OM is used to signify older women and older men, over the age of 40, respectively. Younger women and younger men, under the age of 40, are designated by the letters YW and YM, respectively.

AGENDA DIFFERENCES

To answer our first question, about differences between men's and women's agendas, we looked at replies to a series of 21 open-ended questions that asked panelists to state (a) issues personally most important to them, (b) issues they discussed most frequently, and (c) issues they thought were most important to the general public in their area. Table 2–1 presents the data.

The table shows that basic agenda patterns were quite similar for men and women. Economic issues, such as inflation, taxes, government spending and unemployment, were at the top of the personal, talk and public agendas of both sexes. Social problems, such as welfare programs for the poor, the plight of the elderly, education, health care and crime were next, with young women showing most concern with these issues and young men the least. For the older age groups of both sexes, foreign affairs and defense problems ran third. A check of the media information supply available to our panel shows that all of these issues were amply covered by press and television, al-

TABLE 2-1

Personal, Talk and Public Issue Agendas*
(in percentages; N = 2342 replies.**)

Issue	Personal Agenda				Talk Agenda				Public Agenda			
	OW	YW	YM	OM	OW	YW	YM	OM	OW	YW	YM	OM ***
Social services crime control	15%	16%	10%	14%	17%	21%	10%	15%	10%	11%	9%	12%
Foreign affairs defense	16	8	4	15	7	5	7	11	0	1	1	1
Economy: taxes, jobs, prices	55	65	56	55	43	53	49	40	70	74	71	69
Life styles, race issues	3	7	5	4	2	8	5	2	5	7	5	1
Resource conservation	3	4	8	3	2	1	6	2	2	0	3	1
Feelings about politics	1	0	13	6	2	1	5	6	1	0	1	0
Current political affairs	3	0	2	1	7	2	11	5	5	2	5	7
Miscellaneous & D.K.,N/A.	4	0	2	2	20	10	8	20	6	5	6	8

* Personal agendas indicate issues which respondents rated as personally most important to them; Talk agendas indicate issues which respondents discussed most often; Public agendas indicate issues which respondents consider to be most salient to the general public in their area.
** The N's for personal agenda were : for OW, 281, for YW, 224, for YM, 302 and for OM, 221.
The N's for talk agenda were: for OW, 264, for YW, 214, for YM, 292, for OM, 180.
The N's for public agenda were: for OW, 96, for YW, 84, for YM, 109, for OM, 75.
*** The abbreviations OW and OM stand for older women and men, over age forty; the abbreviations YW and YM stand for younger women and men, under age forty.

beit with somewhat different emphases in each medium. The matches between rank orders of issues in media agendas and in personal agendas were recognizable, but far from perfect.[6]

The data in Table 2–1 indicates that age differences are more significant than sex differences in explaining the minor variations apparent in the personal, public and talk agendas of our four groups.[7] However, a few slight differences between men and women can be detected as well. Women show somewhat greater concern than men about social issues, mentioning them more in their personal and talk agendas. Women also refer more often to economic issues, especially inflation. They talk less about foreign affairs and defense matters than men and show less concern with energy and other resource conservation. Women are also less concerned with problems of national prestige and governmental credibility, and they talk less about current political problems. As mentioned, the differences are slight.[8] However, they conform to the stereotypical views of differences between men's and women's concerns.

A similar picture of only minor distinctions between the sexes emerges when we look at evaluations of issues. Table 2–2 presents a series of issue ratings that our panelists were asked to make, appraising the general importance of these issues and the wisdom of current policies and policy proposals. Importance was rated on a 4-point scale, with 3 points for "very important," 2 points for "somewhat important," 1 point for "not very important" and 0 points for "don't know" answers. Average ratings were computed for each group of issues. They ranged from a score of 2.64 on military spending, marking the great importance that older women attached to that issue, to a score of 1.07 for women's liberation, indicating older men's lack of concern. The numbers of stars indicate the importance of each issue to members of each grouping. Three stars identify the top third, two stars the middle third and one star the bottom range of ratings supplied by panel members.

TABLE 2-2

Importance of Selected Issues and Rank Order of Approval[a]
(N = 3003 replies)

Issue	OW Imp.	OW Appr.	YW Imp.	YW Appr.	YM Imp.	YM Appr.	OM Imp.	OM Appr.
Tax reform	***	1	***	1	***	1	***	1
Government re-organization	***	2	***	2	**	3	**	2
Decentralize power	***	3	**	5	***	4	**	3
Abortion	**	9	*	9	*	5	*	7
Busing	**	10	**	10	**	10	*	10
Amnesty	***	8	**	7	**	6	*	9
Women's equality	**	4	**	3	**	2	*	6
Policy on South Africa	**	7	**	6	**	9	*	8
Policy on Israel	***	5	***	4	***	8	**	5
Military spending	***	6	***	8	***	7	***	4

a *** signifies that the issue rated in the top third of the importance range which went from 2.12 to 2.64 on a scale ranging from 0 to 3.
 ** signifies that the issue rated in the middle third of the importance range which went from 1.59 to 2.11 on a scale ranging from 0 to 3.
 * signifies that the issue rated in the bottom third of the importance range which went from 1.07 to 1.58 on a scale ranging from 0 to 3.

Approval ratings ranked from + 1.52 for tax reform to - 51 for busing on a scale which ranged from +2 to - 2. Scoring methods are explained in the text.

The perceived wisdom of current issues and policies was rated by awarding one or two positive points for mildly and strongly favorable appraisals, respectively, and one or two negative points for mildly and strongly unfavorable ratings, respectively. Unfavorable ratings were subtracted from favorable ratings.

Marked sex distinctions in importance ratings are apparent only for the issue of government reorganization, which was rated as more significant by women than by men. Older women, but not younger ones, also rated amnesty as substantially more important than did older men. All other differences between the sexes were minor.

Approval and disapproval for policies was also quite similar, as seen when we examine the most approved and least approved issues.[9] Plans for tax reform and government reorganization received highest approval rates by both sexes. Busing was awarded the only totally negative score with disapprovals exceeding approvals. Abortion scores rated near the zero point for all panelists, with young men holding the most favorable views of present permissive policies. Women had slightly higher approval rates for U.S. policy toward South Africa and Israel, and slightly less approval of military spending. Again, age differences were more marked than sex differences.

Next we looked at the panelists' perceptions of political candidates to ascertain whether men's and women's agendas of attributes of presidential contenders would differ. Table 2–3 presents the information, based on eleven separate open-ended questions. There are noticeable differences among the images of the three candidates, as described by our respondents, but the differences do not follow gender lines. Both men and women focused on different aspects of the character, style and policy orientation when describing Ford, Carter and Reagan. Ford's experience and aptitude for the presidential office received most attention from all groups, while heaviest emphasis for Carter was on character traits. For Reagan, political philosophy was the area of prime attention.

When one looks with a magnifying glass, some slight gender-related distinctions appear.[10] Women are somewhat more likely than men to express general feelings of like or dislike for the candidates and to mention demographic characteristics like age and occupation. They are less likely to discuss the candidates' political philosophy. Contrary to the stereotypes, their images put a bit more emphasis on the candidates' issue orientations than do those of the men.

However, this does not mean that women generally have a better grasp on issue positions of candidates than do men. Table 2–4 gives an example of the amount of specific information that men and women recalled about the positions taken by Ford and Carter on the

TABLE 2-3

Candidate Attribute Agendas
(percentage of mentions; N = 1407 replies.*)

Area of Comment	Ford				Carter				Reagan			
	OW	YW	YM	OM	OW	YW	YM	OM	OW	YW	YM	OM
General affect	19%	17%	14%	)9%	8%	10%	5%	9%	19%	14%	10%	19%
Honesty/integrity	9	6	6	ა6	5	4	5	8	4	6	6	10
Other character traits	14	12	16	25	18	19	13	17	8	7	4	9
Demographic characteristics	4	4	3	3	9	11	9	3	10	7	10	5
Political orientation	4	8	14	8	7	7	13	7	12	22	29	19
Experience/aptitude	26	18	23	25	10	4	3	11	15	13	7	14
General style	9	6	11	6	13	7	13	11	9	3	6	4
Campaign style	7	8	2	7	14	6	11	13	7	13	9	10
Issue orientation	6	15	7	7	6	20	20	6	8	7	9	4
D.K.	3	6	5	4	10	12	9	15	8	9	9	7

* The N's for Ford agendas were : for OW, 139, for YW,114, for YM, 151, and for OM, 106.
The N's for Carter agendas were: for OW, 137, for YW, 114, for YM, 149, and for OM, 107.
The N's for Reagan agendas were: for OW, 105, for YW, 87, for YM, 117, and for OM, 81.

key issues of unemployment and inflation. Women gave more "don't know" answers than men, particularly for Ford. They also had fewer statistics at their tongue tips and slightly less information about specifics of actual and proposed policies. Women were slightly ahead only on generalized commentary.[11]

Since agenda formation hinges first of all on the availability of news about certain issues, and subsequently on the attention given to this information and on its evaluation, we inquired about the panelists' awareness of news coverage of 40 issues. All of these issues had received substantial coverage in the media to which our core panel members had been exposed. We asked the panelists to indicate, to the best of their knowledge, which of the 40 issues had received a lot of coverage, moderate coverage, or no coverage at all. Table 2–5 lists those issues that panelists rated as having received a lot of coverage. One star means that from 1 to 25% of the answers indicated a lot of coverage; two stars mean that 26 to 50% of the answers gave this indication; three stars mark the 51 to 75% range; 4 stars the 76 to 100% range.

TABLE 2-4

Recall of Specific Information on Unemployment and Inflation*
(in percentages, N = 1716 replies)

Unemployment

Responses	Ford				Carter			
	OW	YW	YM	OM	OW	YW	YM	OM
Statistics	0%	0%	0%	2%	4%	0%	2%	11%
Policy data	12	8	9	12	3	4	3	5
General information	41	38	44	43	43	41	48	35
Don't know	47	55	47	43	50	55	46	48

Inflation

Responses	Ford				Carter			
	OW	YW	YM	OM	OW	YW	YM	OM
Statistics	1%	0%	1%	0%	0%	0%	1%	0%
Policy data	1	2	2	0	3	2	6	6
General information	38	34	39	42	34	29	29	27
Don't know	59	63	59	58	63	69	64	67

*"Statistics" signifies that the respondent was able to cite precise figures for unemployment and inflation rates and/or rate changes. "Policy data" means that the respondent was able to refer to specific proposals made by Ford or Carter to cope with the inflation or unemployment problem.
"General information" means that the respondent knew whether general trends were changing or stable, and knew whether action was planned , without being able to give specifics.

The most striking fact that emerges from Table 2–5 is that panelists varied widely in their perceptions of the frequency with which the media had covered key issues, despite the sameness of coverage trends in their information supply. When one compares ratings for three levels—a lot, moderate and no coverage—only 8% of the issues received similar ratings by the bulk (75% or more) of all replies.

Men's and women's appraisals differed substantially (by 3 or more in the sum of stars) in a number of areas. Women, as a group, noticed more stories about world food problems, health care, malpractice, alcohol and drug addiction, abortion, individual rights, equal rights for women and dirty campaigning. Most of these issues are

TABLE 2-5

Memory of Frequency of Media Coverage of Selected Issues: Percent of Reports of "a lot" of Coverage (N = 840 replies.)[a]

Issue	OW	YW	YM	OM
Welfare	***	**	**	--
Pollution	--	--	*	--
Taxes	**	***	***	--
Elderly/Pensions	**	*	**	*
Crime	**	*	**	**
Govt. credibility	--	****	****	*
Govt. spending	**	****	***	***
Govt. size	**	***	**	**
Energy policy	**	*	**	*
Unemployment	***	****	***	**
Education	**	*	**	--
Inflation	*	****	***	**
Middle East	***	**	**	**
Africa	***	*	**	**
Foreign aid	*	**	**	*
Personal income	*	*	**	--
Unions	*	*	*	*
Environment	*	*	*	--
National defense	*	****	***	***
Big Business	**	**	**	--
Health care	****	--	*	--
Communism	**	**	**	*
Busing	****	**	****	***
Individual rights	**	**	*	--
Urban problems	*	*	*	*
Poverty	**	*	*	--
General economy	****	****	****	***
Race problems	***	--	**	*
Overpopulation	*	--	--	--
Housing	***	--	--	*
Equal rights	***	--	--	--
World food needs	**	**	*	--
Malpractice	****	*	*	*
Alcohol/drugs	****	--	--	*
Abortion	***	**	**	--
U.S. prestige	***	***	***	*
Dirty campaigning	*	***	--	--
Quality of life	*	--	**	*
Corruption	****	***	***	**
City bankruptcy	**	--	--	*

a * signifies that from 1-25% of the answers say "a lot" of coverage.
  ** signifies that from 26-50% of the answers say "a lot" of coverage.
 *** signifies that from 51-75% of the answers say "a lot " of coverage.
**** signify that from 76-100% of the answers say "a lot" of coverage.

traditionally considered as "women's topics." However, this apparent
sex-related differential needs to be appraised in light of the fact that
the bulk of differences between men and women arose because older
men, as a group, were comparatively inattentive to media coverage of
a sizable number of issues. A comparison of women's scores with
those of young men only shows few differences in attention patterns.

While a larger proportion of women remembered seeing or hearing a lot about various topics (26 three- or four-star issues compared
to 14 for men), their ability to recall specific facts was more limited.
Table 2–6 compares sex groupings on the basis of ability to recall facts
about stories. An average of 25% of the males and 38% of the females

TABLE 2-6

**Average Recall of News Stories
(in percentages; N = 5421 stories) ***

	OW	YW	YM	OM
None	33%	42%	29%	20%
Little (one fact)	32	26	17	24
Some (two facts)	23	20	23	23
Lot (three or more facts)	13	13	32	33

* The N's for stories were: for OW, 1351, for YW, 1215, for YM, 1879, for
OM, 976.

recalled no facts at all. Young women contributed heavily to this poor
showing on factual recall. Women also did poorly at the positive end
of the scale. While 33% of the men could recall 3 or more specific
facts about stories on which they were tested, only 13% of the women
remembered "a lot."[12]

Table 2–7 provides comparative data on recall of specific items.
On an average, men recalled specific details for 14% of the new
stories for which we tested them, compared to 5% for women. Even
on the eight issues listed in table 2–7, which were selected because of
their presumed special appeal for women, men's recall of specifics was
substantially better on all but general economic issues.[13]

Tables 2–8 and 2–9 indicate, in rank order, the reasons for remembering stories and for forgetting them.

Table 2–8 shows that women generally lacked focused interests,
such as gathering information to help with their jobs or to learn more
about familiar people. Rather, women tended to remember stories
because they were generally interesting, or touching or appealing.
Often it required multiple exposure before the stories were committed to memory. The poorer recall performance of women may be

TABLE 2-7

Percent of Stories for Which Specific Details
Were Recalled
(for N's, see Table 26)

Story topic	OW	YW	YM	OM
Women's issues	0%	4%	8	20
Medical/health care	2	2	19	9
Education	6	2	11	6
Economy in general	3	3	2	0
Unemployment	13	5	9	15
Inflation	8	3	8	14
Celebrities	18	4	13	18
Entertainment	0	10	14	16
All news stories (including group above)	5	4	14	13

related to the fact that women are less aware of needing information for specific purposes and that their motivation for acquiring it and remembering it is therefore reduced.[14]

However, when women are asked why they fail to remember some stories, they do not generally say that they have little need for them. As Table 2–9 shows, stated reasons for memory failure were quite similar for the sexes, with general inattention and lack of interest rated at the top. The only noticeable difference between the sexes is that men excluded stories more often from attention because they were skeptical about the correctness of the subject matter.[15]

Since the bulk of our recall data had involved recall of specific news stories selected by the investigator, we decided to check our respondents' diaries to see what kinds of stories were recalled spontaneously. The array was wide, with no single type of story predomina-

TABLE 2-8

Reasons for Remembering Stories: Rank
Order of Frequency (for N's see Table 2-6)

Reasons	OW	YW	YM	OM
Job related content			1	5
General importance	1	3	2	1
Shocking content	5	1	3	3
Familiar person	4	4	4	2
General interest	2	2	6	4
Multiple exposure	8	6	7	9
Personally important	3	7	5	7
Appealing presentation	7	5	8	6
Human interest	6	8	9	8
Special interest area	9			
Follows prior story		9		

TABLE 2-9

Reasons for Failure to Remember Stories: Rank Order of Frequency (for N's see Table 2-6)

Reasons	OW	YW	YM	OM
Failed to see/hear story	1	1	1	1
Not interested	2	2	2	2
Too busy	4	4	3	4
Boring story	5	5	5	3
Distrust of media		8	6	
Not important	3	3	4	
Too complex	6	7	7	5
Skeptical about subject		6	8	6
Forgot story	7		9	

ting. For example, 6.2% of 6,000 diary stories dealt with individual crime, 3.6% with accidents, 2.5% with local government, 2.2% with economic issues, 1.8% with the Middle East, 1.7% with Congress, 1.5% with state government, 1.1% with women's issues.

Table 2–10 presents data on the comparative frequencies of mention of selected stories in our respondents diaries. The grouping includes issues ranked high on the panelists personal agendas and issues presumably of special interest to women. Table 2–11 completes the picture by reporting the comparative frequency with which men and women cited certain reasons as prompting them to record stories in their diaries.

Neither table records any major gender-related differences. Men and women paid approximately the same amount of attention to various issues, even those deemed of particular interest to women.[16] (A check of diary data for such "men's topics" as defense and foreign policy shows the same pattern.) Health issues, celebrities and entertainment were most frequently included in the diaries of both sexes and account for slightly over half of all diary entries in the issue groupings presented here. Women showed somewhat more interest, proportionately, in women's issues, while men slightly favored stories about environmental problems.

Among reasons cited for remembering stories for diary entries, general interest and human interests were mentioned most often by both sexes, with emphasis on human interest particularly high for women. Women also mentioned personal importance of a story more often, proportionately, than men. Overall the rank order of frequency of mention of various reasons was fairly similar for men and women, but a comparison of absolute frequencies showed signifi cant differences (p ∠.001).

TABLE 2-10

Diary Entries for Selected Topics: in Percentage and Top Ranks
(N = 1633 stories)*

Issues	OW %	Rank	YW %	Rank	YM %	Rank	OM %	Rank
Women's Issues	5		6		3		3	
Environment	2		2		9	(5)	6	
Medical/Health Care	23	(1)	19	(1)	16	(2)	22	(1)
Religion	3		4		2		5	
Education	10	(4)	5		8		6	
Social Issues	3		8	(5)	5		5	
Economy	9		6		7		10	(4)
Consumer Protection	1		3		3		2	
Celebrities	18	(2)	18	(2)	16	(3)	18	(2)
Entertainment	17	(3)	17	(3)	20	(1)	15	(3)
Human interest	10	(5)	12	(4)	12	(4)	9	(5)

* The N's for diary stories were : for OW, 560, for YW, 237, for YM, 551, and for OM, 285.

TABLE 2-11

Reasons for Remembering Diary Stories: in Percentages and
Top Ranks
(for N's see Table 2-10)

Reason	OW %	Rank	YW %	Rank	YM %	Rank	OM %	Rank
General interest	24	(2)	67	(1)	60	(1)	61	(1)
Entertaining story	10	(4)	2		7	(3)	7	(4)
Human interest	28	(1)	17	(2)	12	(2)	11	(3)
Special interest	10	(5)	6	(3)	6	(4)	4	(5)
General importance	15	(3)	3	(5)	6	(5)	12	(2)
Personal importance	9		4	(4)	4		3	
Job related content	0		0		3		0	
Social life use	1		0		0		1	
Appealing format	0		0		1		1	
Chance	2		0		2		0	

THE INFORMATION SUPPLY

Thus far we have shown that women and men differ very little in their news agendas, in the images and appraisals that they form from their exposure to news, and in their patterns of remembering and forgetting. Aside from the weaker showing on recall of specific details, the data belie the image of women as political primitives. One might argue, however, that women are indeed politically primitive because they fail to focus heavily on issues that are of special concern to them. On these issues, informed opinions by women could be a potent political influence. Before condemning women for this type of primitivism, we need to inquire whether the media presented an adequate supply of women's topics so that women could have included them in their agendas. We also need to look, generally, at the correspondence of media agendas to the agenda of topics to which media audiences pay attention.

To answer this, our second major question, we must turn to our content analysis data. Table 2–12 shows the proportionate coverage given by the *Chicago Tribune* and NBC network and local television news for the same issues selected earlier for diary analysis. Data from the other papers and television news programs analyzed for this study have been omitted to keep the information manageable. However, the data presented in table 2–12 are typical enough of the media covered in our content analysis to be taken as representative of newspaper and local and national television news.

It is apparent from Table 2–12 that there is substantial correspondence between the patterns of attention exhibited by the media and by the diaries (Table 2–10). Women's topics are low on the totem pole of attention for media as well as for media audiences. Three out of the five issues most frequently covered in the *Tribune*—celebrities, human interest stories and health issues—are also leading issues in the diaries. However, the economy and education, which received frequent coverage in the *Tribune,* accounted for comparatively less coverage in the diaries. Conversely, entertainment issues received a lot of attention in the diaries but were comparatively less frequent in the *Tribune.* Comparing national and local television news coverage with diary stories, we again find three issues that rank high in frequency of mention in the media as well as in the diaries. They are health issues, human interest stories and entertainment news. The diaries did not share the heavy emphasis on the economy and environmental issues evident in national television news broadcasts, and the heavy emphasis on education and consumer protection in local television newscasts.[17]

A comparison between media and diary content calls attention to two major facts about the relation between coverage of news and its impact on the minds and memories of news consumers. First, agenda-setting by the media varies in potency; it works more strongly for some issues than for others. The diary rankings in Table 2–10 and the issue rankings in Table 2–5 indicates areas in which the effect seems to be strong; frequency of media coverage is matched by frequency of mention by the media audience. Secondly, the data indicate that even issues receiving comparatively lesser coverage by the media may soar to the top in the public's attention. Once a threshhold of coverage is reached for an issue, the audience's recall may be very high, irrespective of the topic's ranking on media agendas. The coverage of enter-

TABLE 2-12

Coverage of Selected Issues by Chicago Tribune and NBC National and Local News in percentages and all ranks for frequency and prominence scores
(N = 7235 Tribune stories, 1350 NBC national news stories, and 3269 NBC local news stories)

Issues	Tribune			NBC National**			NBC Local		
	PR*	FR*	%	PR	FR	%	PR	FR	%
Women's Issues	8	9	4%	6	10	3%	3	10	3%
Environment	11	8	5%	1	5	10%	7	8	5%
Medical/Health Care	4	5	11%	7	1	18%	4	2	17%
Religion	1	10	4%	5	9	4%	8	11	2%
Education	10	4	12%	2	8	6%	10	3	11%
Social Issues	9	7	8%	4	7	8%	6	9	3%
Economy	3	2	14%	9	3	13%	8	7	7%
Consumer Protection	6	11	2%	3	11	3%	5	4	10%
Celebrities	2	1	16%	11	6	10%	11	6	8%
Entertainment	5	6	11%	10	4	12%	1	5	9%
Human interest	7	3	13%	8	2	13%	2	1	26%

* PR means prominence ranking. For computation, see text.
  FR means frequency ranking. For computation, see text.
** TV coding for national news based on 9 months only, April to December, 1976.

tainment topics is an example where rankings on audience recall agendas far exceeding rankings on media agendas.

Since the "frequency of mention" criterion is a somewhat slender reed on which to lean in judging emphasis on various stories, assorted display features that give prominence to news stories were also examined. For the newspapers, these were page and section number of stories, the presence or absence of pictures and their size, the size of headlines and the length of stories. For television news, they were the time span allotted to a story, the presence or absence of a headline announcing the story early in the program and the use of film to illustrate the story. Table 2–12 includes data on the prominence given to various types of stories. The ratings are based on rank averages computed from composite scores of all prominence factors assessed for press and television stories.[18] Using combined rankings for the three media, women's issues were at the midpoint of prominence ratings for the topics listed in Table 2–12.

The rank order of prominence ratings in tables 2–12 and 2–13 reveal a lack of correspondence between frequency and prominence criteria. What is most frequently mentioned is not necessarily most prominently featured, and vice versa. The tables also show that television and newspaper information supply was more similar in the frequency with which certain issues were featured than in the prominence assigned to them. We do not know what the consequences of these patterns are on agenda-setting.

Apparently, there was no significant relationship between prominence ratings and audience recall. Low prominence ratings did not prevent certain types of stories, such as human interest stories, from capturing the attention of our panelists, nor did high prominence scores, such as those for religious issues, assure public attention. The relationship between frequency of mention in the media and diary mention was somewhat stronger, though it did not reach statistical significance.

That prominence factors have less impact on personal agenda formation than frequency of mention is also apparent from data that we collected on reading patterns by asking respondents to mark all parts of the paper that had come to their attention during a reading session. We found that, depending on the panelist's particular interests and priorities, back pages, short stories and stories with miniscule headlines often received much greater attention than stories displayed more prominently. Given the fact that prominence of display has little effect on the attention bestowed on stories, the fact that women's issues received comparatively prominent coverage was not likely to enhance their impact on male and female audiences.

The relatively low frequency and moderate prominence ratings of "women's issues" prompted us to probe whether specific items, hidden under this umbrella classification, might be trivial and uninteresting and therefore not worthy of special attention by politically sophisticated women. Table 2–13 provides the breakdown for "women's issues" for the *Tribune* and for television stories. (To obtain a workable data base, we had to combine stories from all the television networks.) The table shows that the bulk of issues was hardly trivial. All topics ranked as highly timely and significant by major women's organizations in the United States were included.

TABLE 2-13

Topics of "Women's Issues" Stories in the Chicago Tribune and on Television in percentages and all ranks for frequency and prominence scores*
(N = 179 for *Tribune*, 180 for television)

Issues	Tribune			Television		
	PR	FR**	%	PR	FR	%
Work force discrimination (pay, job rights, benefits	1	1	21%	10	2	20%
Life role changes in military clergy, etc.	5	2	16%	11	1	35%
Miscellaneous civil rights issues	10	3	15%	1	5	6%
Equal Rights Amendment	7	4	13%	7	7	4%
Women in political office	3	5	8%	8	4	7%
Abortion/right to life	8	6	7%	5	3	11%
Credit discrimination/insurance	2	7	6%	6	10	2%
General human interest stories related to women	6	8	4%	4	11	2%
Crime : rape, wife abuse, child abuse	9	9	4%	3	9	3%
Women's organizations: NOW, League, Rape Central, etc.	4	11	3%	9	6	6%
Miscellaneous: sex scandals, medical issues, etc.	11	10	3%	2	8	4%

----

*TV scores based on all networks combined. 12 months coding for local news, 9 months for national news
** PR means prominence ranking. For computation, see text.
   FR means frequency ranking. For computation,=see text.

Since the media did cover important issues, one could reasonably have expected a focus on women's issues in women's diaries. The fact that these issues were comparatively scarce should not have been a bar to attention by women, given the finding that audiences routinely give greater attention to some issues than the media do. That women failed to focus on these issues therefore reveals a lack of political sophistication by a disadvantaged group that has not yet learned to adequately monitor its special interests. It would also have been reasonable to expect ampler and more prominent coverage of these issues by the media. Whether that would have made them more prominent on personal and talk agendas and in the diaries, is, of course, uncertain. It would, however, have made higher rankings on women's agendas more likely.

THE SOCIAL BASIS FOR AGENDA-SETTING PATTERNS

We are now ready to assess the background and current social setting factors that may explain the differences we have noted between agenda formation in men and women. These differences, as shown thus far, are primarily in the nature of the information possessed about various issues, rather than in the range of issues to which attention is given and the importance ratings assigned to them. Women recall less information than men and are less specific in their comments and descriptions about the information that they recall. They put only slightly more emphasis on women's issues than do men, recalling and mentioning them a bit more frequently.

Analysis of background data on our panels shows that men's greater alertness to politics goes back to childhood.[19] Of the men in our core panel, 50%, as compared to 40% of the women, reported substantial interest in politics by their childhood families, including themselves. Men recalled more than twice as many specific political incidents from their childhood years, covering a much wider issue spectrum than women.[20] Wars and elections were remembered by both sexes, but beyond these topics, women tended to stick to local issues and general economic concerns, while men remembered a broad spectrum of national and international happenings.

The sexes reported no difference in availability of media in the home, but men recalled using them more. Both sexes remembered that, compared to their fathers, their mothers made little use of mass media for political information. Our women panelists thus had role models that conformed to the stereotype of low interest in politics, a minor role in political discussions and only fleeting attention to political news.

Turning to current life styles, 25% of the older men and 43% of the younger men reported that their interest in politics was currently high; women expressed interest at lower levels only. Women reported less discussion of current affairs on the job and during leisure hours, and with their families, than did men. They were less able than men to recall specific areas of discussion. While men reported that about half of their discussions were on a serious level, women did not rate any of their discussions as "serious."

Table 2–14 provides data on high levels of media use by men and women. While women reported regular daily use of papers and television slightly more often than men, men used newspapers substantially more for news about politics. This means reduced learning opportunities for women, since recent research indicates that newspapers are the best source for learning specifics about politics, while television is generally a poor source.[21] To compound the learning problem, only 20% of the women read newspapers for more than an hour daily, while 59% of the men did. Of the men, 41% read systematically, without skipping around; none of the women did so. However, 80% of the women, compared to 66% of the men, claimed to pay full attention, without distractions, while reading.

Background and social-setting factors thus provide several plausible explanations for the minor differences in the uses that women and men make of media information. In fact, these factors would justify expectations of far greater differences. We do find these differences, but not in real life. We find them in the females that inhabit women's imaginations. This became clear when we asked our panelists to indicate how frequently they exposed themselves to various types of media stories. Table 2–15 contains the answers. In this self-evaluation, women expressed far heavier interest than men in human interest stories, in crime and accident tales and in features covering home and

TABLE 2-14

**Panelists Mention of High Media Use:
Self-Appraisal
(in percentages; N = 2371 replies)**

Media Usage	OW	YW	YM	OM
Read paper nearly every day	87%	63	70	70
Watch TV news nearly every day	75	49	54	65
Use paper a lot for political news	40	18	40	38
Use TV a lot for political news	43	34	42	37

TABLE 2-15

High Frequency of Exposure to Various Types of Stories in Press and on TV
(N = 168 replies)[a]

Type of Story	Press OW	TV	Press YW	TV	Press YM	TV	Press OM	TV
Human interest	***	**	***	***	***	***	*	--
National politics	*	**	*	***	**	**	***	**
State/Local politics	**	**	--	**	**	***	*	**
People in community	**	--	**	--	***	**	--	--
International affairs	--	*	--	*	**	**	****	***
Home and garden news	*	*	**	--	--	--	--	--
Crime and accidents	**	***	***	****	**	***	*	--
Editorials	--	*	--	****	***	*	*	*

a   * signifies that from 1-25% of the answers report high frequency of exposure.
  ** signifies that from 26-50% of the answers report high frequency of exposure.
  *** signifies that from 51-75% of the answers report high frequency of exposure.
  **** signifies that from 76-100% of the answers report high frequency of exposure.

garden information. They expressed slim interest in international politics, and less interest than men in general national, state and local political affairs.

We have shown that the data on women's agendas, on story recall and on diary entries do not bear out the skewed patterns depicted by this self-assessment. Similarly, other scholars who have reviewed the social-scientific evidence on sex-based differences in political information and attitudes have concluded that "virtually all investigations show no political differences between men and women that can be attributed to the factor of sex itself. . . . Even on questions directly related to sex distinctions, differences between men and women are neither large nor consistent."[22]

Nonetheless, the stereotype of women as political primitives who avoid political information continues to live. It gains some support from women's behavior in assimilating precise information and from their neglect of important sex-linked issues. It thrives on the fact that women talk less about current political affairs and express less interest in them. It manifests itself strongest of all in women's voiced self-appraisals.[23]

This is the crucial place where the stereotype must first be laid to rest. Women must realize that politics concerns them as much as men. Not only must they continue to watch the same issues as men, but they must watch them with equal attention to detail. Women must also become more aware of the role they must play in pressuring for policies that advance women's interests. This requires greater attention to news concerning women's issues.

Once the stereotype of women as political primitives has been laid to rest, the media, ever anxious to supply the interested public with what it wants to read and hear, are bound to give better coverage to issues that are of great concern to their female audiences. If women are perceived as alert to the news and as major contributors to public opinion, the media, as well as the political world, will reflect greater respect for women's political interests and power.

NOTES

[1] Bonnie Cook Freeman, "Power, Patriarchy, and 'Political Primitives,'" in Joan Roberts, ed., *Beyond Intellectual Sexism* (New York: David McKay, 1976), pp. 231–40. Also see Virginia P. Richmond and James C. McCroskey, "Whose Opinion Do You Trust?" *Journal of Communication,* 25 (Summer 1975), pp. 42–50.

[2] Collaborators for the content analyses as well as the interview data were Professor Maxwell McCombs of Syracuse University and Professor David Weaver of Indiana University and their associates. Each investigator and their associates was responsible for data collected in her/his geographical location. Data on sample selection are available from all collaborators.

[3] The *Chicago Tribune* and the *Lebanon Valley News* were content-analyzed on a daily basis for six days per week to reflect the full information supply as closely as possible. For the Indiana papers, every fourth day was coded, including Sundays. The *Daily News* and *Sun Times* were used primarily as comparisons for *Tribune* coverage. The local broadcasts were coded directly from the actual broadcast event. The network newscasts were analyzed from written abstracts prepared by the staff of the Vanderbilt Television News Archives. Comparison of control codings taken from the actual broadcast with abstract-codings showed no significant differences for the type of coding relevant here. The reliability of coding for the content analyses was carefully checked and controlled. Since many different coders were involved in this project, it is difficult to report a single reliability figure. Our procedure was to have the same coding supervisor check each coder's work following the initial training period, and at various intervals thereafter. Excluding simple identification categories, like paper or station name and date, which would inflate reliability figures, intercoder reliability averaged 85% and intracoder reliability averaged 90%.

[4] John W. Soule and Wilma E. McGrath, "A Comparative Study of Male-Female Political Attitudes at Citizen and Elite Levels," pp. 178–95 in Marianne Githens and Jewel Prestage, *A Portrait of Marginality: The Political*

Behavior of the American Woman (New York: David McKay, 1977), which identifies women's issues.

[5] Generational changes are discussed in Gerald Pomper, *Voters' Choice: Varieties of American Electoral Behavior* (New York: Dodd, Mead & Co., 1975), pp. 90–118. Also note sources cited there.

[6] For examples of matches, compare tables 2–10 and 2–12.

[7] For similar data, see Pomper, cited in note 5.

[8] Chi-square significance tests for the chief agenda topics (Social services/crime control and Economy: taxes, jobs, prices) showed no significant differences between men and women for personal and public agendas. For talk agendas, the significance of differences was in the .05 to .02 range.

[9] Spearman's rho between men's and women's appraisal scores was .94 for OW-OM scores; .93 for OW-YW scores; .77 for YW-OM scores; .76 for OW-YM scores; .72 for YW-YM scores; .70 for YM-OM scores; all for $N = 10$.

[10] Using chi-square, the differences between women and men were not significant for Carter and Reagan. For Ford, the significance of differences was in the .05 to .02 range.

[11] The differences between women and men were statistically significant only for information on Carter's unemployment policies (.05 to .02 range).

[12] These differences between women and men are significant at the .001 level, using chi-square.

[13] These differences between women and men are significant at the .001 level, using chi-square.

[14] The importance of goal-oriented information seeking is discussed in Charles Atkin, "Instrumental Utilities and Information Seeking," pp. 205–42 in Peter Clarke, ed., *New Models for Mass Communication Research* (Beverly Hills, Calif.: Sage Publications, 1973). Spearman's rho between women's and men's recall reason scores was .83 for YM-OM scores; .76 for OW-YW scores; .73 for YW-OM scores; .70 for OW-YM scores; .42 for YW-YM scores; all for $N = 11$.

[15] Spearman's rho between women's and men's forgetting scores was .92 for YW-YM scores; .91 for OW-YW scores; .90 for OW-YM scores; .72 for YW-OM scores; .72 for YM-OM scores; .69 for OW-OM scores; all for $N = 9$.

[16] For corroborating data, see Pomper, cited in note 5, pp. 67–89 and sources cited there. There are no statistically significant differences between men's and women's diary entries when the three top-ranked issues (medical/health care, celebrities, entertainment) are examined.

[17] Consumer protection ranked higher than average for NBC local news because of special programming featuring consumer protection on a regular basis. For complementary data on frequency and substance of coverage of women's topics, see E. Terrence Jones, "Women and Public Policy: The Role of the Press" (Southwestern Political Science Association paper, 1976).

[18] The scoring for and impact of various display characteristics is discussed in Richard W. Budd, "Attention Score: A Device for Measuring News 'Play'," *Journalism Quarterly*, 41 (1964), pp. 259–62.

[19] The literature on the effects of early sex role socialization is large and con-

troversial. See, for example, Anthony M. Orun, *etal.*, "Sex Socialization and Politics," *American Sociological Review,* 39 (April 1974), pp. 197–209, and sources cited there. Also Kirsten Amundsen, *The Silenced Majority* (Englewood Cliffs, N.J.: Prentice Hall, 1971); Virginia Sapiro, "Socialization to Political Gender Roles Among Women" (Midwest Political Science Association Paper, 1977), and "News from the Front: Inter-Sex and Inter-Generational Conflict over the Status of Women" (APSA paper, 1977).

[20] This is particularly true of younger men.

[21] E.g., see Sidney Kraus and Dennis Davis, *The Effects of Mass Communication on Political Behavior* (University Park: Pennsylvania State University Press, 1976), pp. 48–109. The significance of media use differences between men and women is in the .10 to .05 range, using chi-square.

[22] Pomper, cited in note 5, pp. 67–68. For evidence that well-educated women of high socio-economic status behave with the same degree of political sophistication as men, see Robert D. Putnam, *The Comparative Study of Political Elites* (Englewood Cliffs, N.J.: Prentice Hall, 1976), p. 33; Susan Welch, "Women as Political Animals? A Test of Some Explanations for Male–Female Differences," *American Journal of Political Science,* 21 (1977), pp. 711–30; Lynda Watts Powell, "Male and Female Contributors to the 1972 Presidential Election" (Midwest Political Science Association paper, 1977).

[23] Psychological aspects of sex role typing are discussed in Barry Bozeman *et.al.*, "Continuity and Change in Opinions about Sex Roles," in Prestage and Githens, cited in note 4, pp. 38–65. Also see Richard G. Niemi, *How Family Members Perceive Each Other* (New Haven: Yale University Press, 1974), pp. 66–68.

III

Women Out of the Myths and Into Focus

by **PATRICIA RICE**

St. Louis Post-Dispatch

FIRST OF ALL, without a whit of disagreement with fellow author Maxwell McCombs, I would like to assure you romantic newspaper addicts that the women and men of the press have not become so high brow that they run around talking about the press's agenda-setting function.

Agenda-setting? I tested the word on ten colleagues, reporters and editors from six papers stretched from the *New York Times* to the *Honolulu Advertiser*. Not one gave the same definition that McCombs did when he coined it five years ago. Most came nowhere close.

The cigar smoking has diminished in the city rooms, spitoons have been moved out and the computer's visual display terminals have been moved in. We may have clean floors and walls painted in colors, yes, real colors like red, pink and blue. But in city rooms, *newsworthy* is still the word we use. It defines what goes into the paper.

Editors and reporters who are responsible for a beat do worry about what news we find room for. We know that a newspaper can only handle so many inches of ideas, so many reports from all the events of one day in our city, state and world. Those who communicate over radio and television have a harder problem: squeezing the news into the word-equivalent of less than one-half of a standard-size newspaper front page in every half hour of broadcast.

Sure we know that most international crises fester long before they become front page news. Before the women demonstrate, before the diplomat is kidnapped, the archduke shot. We know that to mention one philosophy and not another, one style of blue grass guitar-picking and not another, one Japanese restaurant and not another, one rotten-apple bureaucrat and not another, one woman who is first in her industry and not another presents only part of life. But, we hope the more newsworthy part.

And, if you think we don't know about the other philosophy, guitar-picker, and so on, answer our phones. We know fast. A couple of hours after the paper hits the street calls come in to say they want "equal time" for the problems of the sanitation department of for Uncle Clem who plays guitar, claw-hammer style.

As citizens of your community, the press decides what we think you will need or want to know to be good voters, taxpayers, residents, consumers, parents, employers and employees and just thoughtful creative persons, as well as the person who woke up in the middle of the night wondering where all the fire engines were going.

And, more and more now, the press, in order to stay in the black, calls on academics and researchers like Dr. Graber to survey readers about what they say they want to read. So today, newspapers come up with extras. Not news extras of the past, but color tabloids: on consumerism, on what to do with leisure time, on what to wear and where to eat and on personalities. And since they sell papers, they help put papers in the black and, in a way, bring you the hard news.

With all these extras, it would seem that there would be more serious news about women. And some say there is.

But in February, 1976 the AAUW, the American Association of University Women found, as a result of a national study of newspapers, that there was less news coverage of women after women's pages were given up. Complaints have come from all sides. *She* magazine polled 5,000 women in 1976 and found them overwhelmingly dissatisfied with the coverage of women's news. Hundreds of local and regional women's newspapers have sprung up because women's news in big papers is not providing information. The quality and news in much of these is less than objective. Most are in the American tradition of the political pamphlet. And a vice-president of UPI recently called for his wire service to do a better job of covering women's news.

In newsrooms across the country, women reporters monitor the news. They race to editors to expunge a reference to Golda Meir as a "grandmother premier." They tease male reporters into equality in writing with critiques on the bulletin board. Some have formalized coalitions to get more and better news about women into their papers and onto their station's airwaves. In several EEOC suits, newswomen have not only charged their employers with a bias in employment but a bias in reporting women's news.

So it does not surprise me that Dr. Graber's recent research has shown us that women remember different things from newspapers than men do, or that women more often fail to relate the news to their own life and their own chances of advancement.

Graber's women grew up or lived through the 1950s, when the women in the news were jailed on a page or two of the daily paper. Sometimes just a column or two. The Women's Page. And unreal women at that. Even then, women loved to read about women. No matter how remote to her life, a woman can identify with a woman. Surveys showed that women devoured those women's pages.

But, an image from the early 1960s burns in my reporter's memory more painfully than any survey. I can remember almost daily seeing middle-aged black women in tattered, second-hand clothes riding the morning bus to factory jobs downtown. They shared a left-behind newspaper. Each day they inevitably turned first to the women's page to read about other women. The stories they found there were mostly about charity events, debuts, trips to resorts and weddings. Stories about wealthy white women they would never meet. But, day after day, the poor women on my bus read that page first. And often not much else.

I can tell you, too, of the wife of a presidential candidate who turned first to a woman's page to read about an elderly woman quilter before she began her serious business of carefully studying the news columns for what her husband had said the day before. I can tell you about a beautifully groomed, bright social leader who could practically recite the story of the "first woman plumber to pass the local union's qualifications."

Dr. Graber found women less interested in international affairs. I wonder what she would have found if she had done her study in the 1940s. People read about what touches them and their lives. How different it must have been when the name of a woman's husband, brother or neighbor might be reported dead or missing on the "War

Page." The women of the early 1940s could recite the names of exotic places where battles were fought and rattle off unit and battalion numbers.

In the 1950s, the women who could detail the battles of Iwo Jima or the landing in Normandy were asked to bring their minds back home. The man in the Gray Flannel suit did not want to talk politics when he returned home. Nor did the blue-collar worker, who discovered the fights on television. McCarthy made international politics—all of it—seem un-American.

Patricia Cayo Sexton wrote an article in 1959 in *Harper's Magazine* called "Speaking for the Working Class Wife," in which she stated: "The House is often a refuge for women. But, escape from life leaves no life at all. Women comply because husband, children and state seem to expect it. But, there is usually at least a wistful longing to break out and a well-founded suspicion that they are missing something important."

In this atmosphere, the woman who decides to devour everything there is to read about the conflicts in Northern Ireland or the Panama Canal Treaty may just have no one with whom to discuss it. How many persons would store up information like a growing ball of used string and just leave it on the "upper shelves" of their mind?

A decade ago, most women worked at home and most newspapers limited women's news to food, social notes and fashion, with only a few intrusions from the other end of the economic spectrum as in "100 Neediest Cases" or in a report on the increase in the number of ADC mothers. It would be easy to accuse the press of allowing women to think that the most important thing on their agenda was to live like Doris Day in *Pillow Talk* or *Teacher's Pet* (Day was the biggest female box-office star from 1959 to 1965).

No paper would, after all, print the real story of life at home. Newsworthy? Imagine such a story.

"Mrs. J. Arthur Smith, known to her friends as Marge, emptied the garbage with precision 11 times this week. She prepared 18 meals, each with portions for five persons. Four of the meals were terrific and one was a terrible-tasting but cheap macaroni casserole. She knitted one and a half socks while spending two days at home waiting for the clothes-dryer repairman to show up. She did seven loads of wash. She dusted the entire house six times, except Tuesday when she forgot to dust the dining room because an Avon Lady interrupted her. She suffers from nagging backache."

End of story.

Women did work outside the home. A decade ago, like today,

most of those women were in unglamorous jobs: the pink-collar workers who labored as waitresses, elevator operators, dental reserva-
tionists, store clerks, nurses aides. Hard work but with far lower wages
than blue-collar jobs. And for a time women's pages did and still do "a
day in the life of . . ." stories on these women and their jobs.

Add to these routine jobs the custom that a lady's name should
not appear in the newspapers but for her birth, wedding and death—
unless she wins the State Fair bake-off or makes a debut.

Less than a decade ago I tried to write an article about a career
woman, an insurance saleswoman, whose civic volunteer work was
also notable. Before she consented to be interviewed, she said she had
to ask her husband. She called me back to say he had said "no." It
would embarrass him to acknowledge to his friends that she worked
for a living. So, if the house is not a refuge for women as Patricia
Cayo Sexton said, it is obvious to this woman's husband that she was
supposed to pretend, at least to his friends, that it was.

They had bought into the myth—which Elizabeth Janeaway states
in her book *Man's World, Woman's Place*—that a woman must be either
a pleasing woman or a shrew.

Then, in the mid-sixties, it became the law of the land that
women had to be given an equal opportunity in employment. Hard to
enforce though it was and is, the number of women going into the job
market increased. They needed jobs; they needed them to keep up
the standards of a family life that the economy set, needed the job to
keep the United States economy charging along. Women graduating
from school began to talk seriously—more seriously than women had
talked since the 1920s—of preparing themselves for careers for life,
not just grabbing something interesting to do until they married.

Which happened first, the chicken or the egg? There was more to
write about women now. There were more women to write about
women. Women's pages edited by women and reported by women
began articles that now could be called one long series of "First
woman does this or that."

And women reporters, tired of wasting their days filling in the
blanks on who was going to which resorts, to whose dinner parties,
grabbed their notebooks and headed for construction sites to write
about the first woman in town to put up a dry wall. The first woman
to be a high school janitor. The first woman to drive a truck.

And suddenly all over the country it seemed that women were
working in blue-collar jobs. The daughters of Rosie the Riveter were
climbing phone poles, delivering mail. And Rosie? Well, she might be
going back to college. The oldest student in physics or assertiveness
training.

At first these newsworthy women were presented like freaks. Just like Elizabeth I, Florence Nightingale or Madame Curie, they were considered accidents of their sex.

But soon it became apparent that the women who went into the mid-sixties' marketplace were not freaks. Yes, they broke the stereotype, lead after lead said. But only because the stereotypes were wrong. They were neither pleasing women nor shrews. They were neither or both and so much more. Women were more complicated than any stereotypes that the newspapers had fenced them into on those women's pages. Reporters on women's pages tried to pull women out of the myths and into focus.

Peace in Vietnam became a woman's news story. Mothers marched for peace. Others took the hawks' side, saying that their son wounded or fallen must not have died in vain. Women spoke out, were arrested, flew to Vietnam, sought the missing in action. The MIA was a women's issue. Its leaders were women.

Ecology news began in many newspapers as a women's issue, as it did at the *Post-Dispatch*. Yes, finally what you did with your sacks of garbage was news. What you sprayed your tomatoes with was news. Cutting back on chauffeuring your kids around town was news. It was news to get your kids hooked on public transportation and on bikes.

What women talked about with fury was news. How they were treated by their gynecologists. In this explosion of women's news, it was not surprising that not a medical writer but a child-care writer at *Family Circle*, Barbara Seaman, wrote a series of articles that became her book *The Doctor's Case Against the Pill*. The story was not broken by the men who covered the medical beats in the country. Seaman and others have continued to study the effects of hormone treatments and have translated hefty medical evidence into readable news stories. Seaman wanted women to be interested and alert. Her third book on hormones was published recently. Those same medical writers rarely emphasized the importance of early detection of breast cancer—until the President's wife and the Vice-President's wife were struck with it—and then the breast cancer story became a national epidemic.

It was on the women's pages that consumerism became big news. Not the old "Heloise Hints" on how to use nylon net for everything, which had been only filler to even up the holes in news columns. Now consumer news was the hard stuff. Like funeral home fraud. Car dealer repair pitfalls.

When Charlotte Curtis, the women's editor of the *New York Times*, was chosen to succeed Harrison Salisbury as editor of the Op-Ed page, eyebrows were raised in some quarters. But Curtis told them that if they had been reading, they would have seen that the women's pages—by then renamed Family or Style sections—were the most interesting parts of the newspapers.

The women's movement—by that I mean the organized groups of women who banded together to gain equal treatment, child care, abortion rights or right to life—pulled average women into the political process. Many of those women had never thought politically before, even though they may have labored in politics making coffee or stuffing envelopes for individuals or issues.

Twelve years ago, a group of upper middle-class women of high achievement sat at a luncheon where a study they had prepared as the President's Commission on the Status of Women was to be heralded. It was obvious to them that LBJ and his administration would bury their labors, their recommendations. They had been given no power to enforce their ideas. But they had been made newsworthy because a president had appointed them. So they decided women would have to ban together to work for their rights. They called themselves the National Organization for Women. NOW. And they went to the press only after they had met in a hotel room after the luncheon. A women's group was news.

After NOW, all kinds of alphabet anagrams of women asked for coverage. And they brought the press their new ideas—ideas their grandmothers and great-grandmothers had also written about to the press wrapped up in a big word. Revolution. And for a while it was newsworthy. And it was a revolution. But, not one glamorous enough for the movies. Or for the press after a while. Especially not glamorous enough for men. Men readers wrote the editors and said it was boring. Men reporters said they never read the woman stuff and certainly were grateful that the woman staff reporters seemed willing to bear the burden of writing about it. Oh, there were some fun things. What could have been more of a media event than women crashing the all-male sanctum of McSorley's bar and its equivalents all over the country. And then there were the photographers. The ones who had taken joy all these years in finding the prettiest girl in a crowd. They went to women's events and now kept bringing their photo editors pictures of the ugliest woman in every parade. And their kind in the television crews who shot only the loudest shrieking paraders. Middle-aged, well-starched feminists might as well have not existed, at least in some newspapers' photographs. Some of those editors seemed to be trying to say all women had to be either pleasing or shrews. Again.

In their attempts to be newsworthy, the leaders of the women's movement often promised too much, too soon. And so when reporters came back to check progress on schedule, they asked if the movement had failed. Or was dead. Or was really a revolution.

One of the most interesting ways to judge the way women are treated in the press is to observe coverage of the political woman. Presumably someone who is willing to sacrifice hundreds of hours from career or homemaking to ring doorbells, run phone blitzes, and talk at every chicken dinner in town is serious and should be treated seriously. It is only fair to the voters as well as to the politicians that someone who is elected, receives wages from our taxes, makes the decision about taxes, war and even which pothole to patch first deserves attention—serious attention.

The first woman elected to serve in Congress was Jeanette Rankin of Montana. The year was 1917, before women in most states could even vote. Congresswoman Rankin pushed through the suffrage amendment and proposed the first maternal and infant health bill in 1921. In the press, Rankin was treated as weird. Like an accident of nature or an Elizabeth I, rather than an equal to other Congressmen. When she voted against a declaration of war against Germany in 1917, 49 other Congressmen joined her. But she was singled out and given a bad time. She retired after a term and did not go back to Congress until 1940. Ironically she again was there for a vote to declare war. This time she did stand alone against the entire Congress in opposing it.

After two decades the press treated her a little better. She was an oddity but from some there was praise. The Kansas *Emporia Gazette* editor, William Allen White wrote: "The *Gazette* entirely disagrees with the wisdom of her position, but, Lord it was a brave thing. And its bravery somehow discounted its folly."

Political women were given a new goal when in 1952 Senator Margaret Chase Smith, a senator for four years and a veteran of four terms in the House, sought the Republican vice-presidential nomination with some 250 delegates pledged to her. Candidate Dwight D. Eisenhower blocked her name from being nominated on the convention floor that year and Richard Nixon became Ike's running mate.

That same year, when she so seriously sought higher office, Senator Smith allowed herself to make a cute joke. When she was asked what would happen if she woke up in the White House one day she replied: "I'd go straight to Mrs. Truman and apologize. Then, I'd go straight home."

No feminist today would allow such cuteness to crack her professional demeanor. But the press loved it; it is a funny quote. And it is better remembered than her brief reach for the vice-presidency.

In the early 1970s, some women thought that they did really get more publicity by being a woman candidate. In interviews with some 50 woman state legislators from 30 states in early 1972, I found that they thought the press treated them well. They could get more public attention by being featured on the women's pages. And they were no longer asked for recipes. However, they resented that news of them was kept in a ghetto. They were rarely written about with men in the news columns. They could achieve some recognition, as freaks, as unusual, or even as a personality on the women's pages, but they could not have the equality of being taken seriously in the news analysis section. The state legislators found that their male counterparts were envious of their name recognition, while unaware of the patronizing lack of attention to women in the news columns. There was one plus. The legislators said that the press, through years of reporting about the clean image, the issue-oriented stance of the League of Women Voters, had helped all women look issue-oriented and honest.

The 1972 elections were a breakthrough year for women in politics. Sissy Farenthold became the first woman seriously nominated for vice-president from a major party convention. Women were nearly one-half of the delegation at the Democratic party's convention and the number of women in Congress increased from 14 to 18. The press treated women more fairly. Women were in the news columns. Real efforts were made to interview women on the floor of the convention. And women voters were solicited seriously. Jane Muskie and Eleanor McGovern talked issues that women were concerned about. Seriously. Both steered clear of recipes.

Any wisecracking politician who decided not to worry about the woman voter was left behind. Women were not just out to vote for the matinee idol male politician. Women in political parties, and especially wives of leading politicians, reminded the politicians of that. Still some political news commentators reduced women to daydreaming Judith Exners. They told us women voted for Kennedy because he was handsome. False. According to George Gallup, the matinee idols have never won the women's vote. Kennedy received only 49% of the women's vote in 1960; Nixon received 51%. Carter generally is thought to be more attractive than Ford. Yet the charisma columnists were wrong again. Ford received 51% of the women's vote, President Carter, 48%. This is underlined by Graber's findings in Table 2–3 that women's issues put a bit more emphasis on the candidates' issue-orientation than male readers do.

In the Spring of 1976, Shirley Chisholm became so frantic about the coverage of her race for the presidency that she sued the networks.

Some feminists complain when women candidates are described physically. This is good reading and acceptable as long as men are described as well.

During the 1976 primary and general election, I participated with nine other reporters in a study of the campaigns of women in ten states. It was backed by the Carnegie Foundation and run by the National Women's Education Fund and Rutgers University Eagleton Center for Women in American Politics. Press coverage of women in politics was often fair in the 1976 campaigns. But, sexism in the races in ten states did exist, and on all levels.

Take Sue Rockne, a teacher, with a Master's degree, a member of a school board with a long track record in community activities. She ran for the Minnesota Senate. And the Minneapolis *Post-Bulletin* referred to her as a Zumbrota (that is her town) housewife. Her opponent was always referred to as a farmer. Rockne refuted the statement by saying her opponent was not, in fact, a farmer, just because he lived on a farm. She said he had no callouses on his hands. Still, in many states when farm women ran, they were almost never referred to as farmers, no matter how much work they did on the land or at the farm's management desk with farm accounts.

Out in Ventura County, California, a newspaper went to the trouble of printing Jane Tolmach's Strawberry Pie recipe—not on a food page—but in the news section. She was running for State Assembly. But, when Governor Jerry Brown showed up to make a public appearance with her, the newspaper ignored it.

As a newspaper woman, I wonder why she used the pie recipe in her campaign literature if she did not want it part of her public image. And, as a newspaper woman, I wonder if time and lack of man- or womanpower prevented that city editor from covering the Brown appearance. A mention of the governor's endorsement would have seemed to be appropriate. Often complaints such as these are really not mistakes by the press.

Probably the most outrageous sexist remark about any of the women in the ten states in the Eagleton study was made in the Cleveland *Plain Dealer* by reporter Robert Daniles. He interviewed the successful candidate from Ohio's Twentieth Congressional District, Mary Rose Oaker. The question and answer format interview was fair until the end of the story. Oaker is single, a teacher, 36-years old. She is religious and of Syrian background. It ended with the unanswered flip question: "By the way, Mary Rose Oaker, how's your love life?" Not even Senator Smith in her most humorous mood would have been amused at that one. And unlike Smith, there seems to be not a breath of scandal about Oaker's love life.

The press gives the public something extra to worry about when it sets another agenda for women candidates by asking the inevitable: "And what will your family do if you are elected to office?"

The question is asked of career women who already cope with home and career as well as of housewives with empty nests. When did anyone ever ask a male candidate about how he could manage as a father and husband and Senator. Have you worried about the children of poor Senator Percy or poor Senator Danforth? According to some reporter's line of questioning, you should consider the fate of the women's children and husband before pulling the voting lever.

Not even Phyllis Schlafly, who claims to fight for the right of women to stay home, does that. The mother of six has run twice unsuccessfully for Congress and is considering a run for the Senate in 1978.

Jean Berg, who ran in the Democratic primary for Congress from Northeastern Missouri in 1976 was plagued by the question. She has two college-age children and a husband who is a college administrator. "I would tell them that Dick would take a sabbatical leave from college and would move with me. That seemed to satisfy those who asked. And Dick would have done it."

Have you ever heard a politician called a divorced husband? Well, Gretchen Kafoury ran for the Oregon legislature and that is what the *Oregonian* of Portland, Oregon, called her when they endorsed her opponent. Moreover, she was called the divorced wife of a former State Representative.

I believe that often many of the complaints women candidates make can be turned back to their own campaign managers. The press was told too late to cover the event, the wrong reporter was called, the reporter you sent the letter to was out of town.

But, some things can not be forgiven. In the September, 1977, *Harper's Magazine,* issue is taken with a cruel photograph of Bella Abzug in the *New York Times* in the middle of her mayoral race. It shot her from below the platform nearly up her skirt. It is the picture of an aging, fat-legged woman. An angle no male politician is shot from.

Some sophisticated women politicians have effectively used the media. A law student at Washington University has received as much media coverage as any woman elected to public office. Phyllis Schlafly, a political columnist, author and two-time Congressional candidate, has continually asked the media to cover "the other side of the ERA movement," even when the other side seemed only to be Mrs. Schlafly and a few in the right wing of the Republican party. She was able to get space on the Op-Ed pages of America for her column giving "the other side to ERA and other issues." She knows how to fall into the old stereotype of the pleasing woman rather than the shrew. And she sees that her image is always pleasing. Before her Stop ERA fight, she wore well-worn, comfy Peck and Peck wools, upper-class tweedy. She has changed her palette to pinks and baby blues with lots of ruffles. She has blonde hair and spit curls. Her old school classmates envy her youthful, carefully groomed "soft and pretty" look. She has also carefully softened the shrill voice that once howled through a Republican Women's national meeting when she was defeated for its presidency and called for a recount. She has polished the manners the nuns taught her at school (and ironically, those nuns politically oppose her today).

She did not ask the press to change. She changed and grabs a lot of publicity because of it. In the May, 1976, issue of *Ms* Magazine, Lisa Cronin Wohl showed that newspapers gave, in fact, more coverage to anti-ERA news than pro-ERA news.

But women don't have to change in this manner. They can continue both outside the newspapers and as reporters inside the newspapers to ask for fair treatment of women in the news. Every faircomplaint letter helps. Editors are sensitive and most editors at big city papers are trying to be fair.

A witty letter goes a lot farther than an angry one. You may know that in some papers there is still a major war going on as to whether a woman can be called Ms. if she choses. It goes on at the *New York Times* and many small papers. In a recent *Quill,* Donald Williams protested the change and pleaded for the maintenance of the old titles on the grounds that he "still cherished his right to express joy in the sight of a pretty knee or waistline or bosom, etc." Melinda J. Whitney, a graduate student at the University of Nevada-Reno responded (one of 16 letters printed in a follow-up issue):

> I find that it is men who are short-changed in the newsprint world. Why should men be deprived of a title or given no choice at all when women have three to choose from? Why not use a convenient Mr. (for married) and M. (for unmarried men), continue the practice of calling women Mrs. or Miss, and drop the whole Ms. issue. This most certainly would bestow upon women and men equal, though not identical, distinction."

More editors can be humored into equality. It may achieve more than the picketing and assaults of the past.

IV

An Overview of Access to the Media

by **EDIE N. GOLDENBERG**
The University of Michigan

WHEN POLITICAL SCIENTISTS talk about access, they usually mean access to elected or appointed officials. This is so, simply because much of the thinking about access grows out of interest group research, which focuses primarily on the interactions between groups of officials.[1] But one can also discuss access to the mass media. The media dispense values of importance to interest groups. For example, the media provide publicity for leaders which in turn provides incentives for their continued involvement in the group; the media attract members by informing them of the group and its activities; they facilitate fund raising by informing interested third parties of the group's activities.[2]

The media also serve as important intermediaries for interest groups. If groups lack direct access to government personnel, they are faced with the problem of trying to influence government indirectly. The media are important to many indirect influence attempts.

50

Through the media, issues and perspectives can be brought to official attention. Some have argued that media coverage can make issues more important to the general public as well.[3] Media attention can help groups win advantages from government and can help the groups themselves survive or even grow for future challenges. Therefore, understanding the factors facilitating and impeding access to the media is important for those interested in how the political system operates.

Understanding access to the media is important for media watchers as well. Since the Hutchins Commission report in 1947, there has been discussion among media watchers and media personnel of the "social responsibility theory of the press."[4] Among other things, this view urges the press to be truthful, complete and accurate, to provide for the exchange of comment and criticism and to present a "representative picture of the constituent groups in society." To the extent that the media system is tilted against certain viewpoints and groups, it is not fulfilling these social responsibilities.

This chapter presents an overview of the concept of access to the press. The overview has three parts. First, the concept is defined. Second, the "accepted wisdom" on the usefulness of confrontation as a media technique for resource-poor groups is discussed. And third, attention is directed toward the newspaper organization and its effect on the ability of resource-poor groups to gain press access.

DEFINITIONS AND DISTINCTIONS

"Access" is used in several different ways. In political science, access usually refers to the ability to get a hearing with someone about an interest or demand. For example, if the leaders of an interest group try to get a hearing with a newspaper reporter and they succeed, then they can be said to have access to that reporter and through that reporter to the newspaper. If they try and fail, then they lack access. Of course, group leaders may not try in the first place, either because they anticipate failure or because they prefer other tactics.[5] With no effort on their part, we cannot assess their ability to get a hearing. Moreover, even if the group does try and does succeed in getting hearing, they may not get what they want. Merely because a reporter listens to group leaders is no guarantee that a story will appear. As in any political situation, groups can be heard and still not prevail. Without this distinction, access and influence become synonymous and superfluous. Consequently, studying access to the press requires considering the behavior of both those seeking a hearing with the press and newspaper personnel.

This has methodological implications. Content analysis, by itself, provides insufficient information from which to answer questions about access to the press. One can conclude neither that coverage indicates access nor that a lack of coverage indicates a lack of access without further information on the activities of news subjects and news personnel. Two recent studies illustrate the point.

The first is Fred Fedler's study of minority group coverage in Minneapolis.[6] It provides a good example for why coverage is not equivalent to access. Fedler found that 20 "minority" groups received as much coverage in local media as did a matched set of "mainstream" groups. From this we might be tempted to conslude that minority groups in Minneapolis have no access problems with the local media. However, Fedler also reported substantial differences in the coverage of mainstream and minority groups. The Minneapolis newspapers published stories about mainstream group endorsements of political candidates, conferences, awards and honors, reports, elections of officers, statements and fund drives. In contast, very similar activities of minority groups received no press coverage. For them, coverage was almost exclusively of confrontations of one kind or another. It appears that minority groups had to engage in activities that were very intense and conflictual before news people would cover them. If such activities are required before news people will pay attention, the activities may overwhelm the message groups are trying to convey. The who, what, where and when may drown out the why, and groups may never have any real opportunity to get their message across. Consequently, one needs to know more than the absolute amount of news coverage before reaching conclusions about the access of various groups to the media.

Once we accept the idea that access and amount of coverage are not usefully regarded as the same thing, we might be tempted to equate access with certain types of coverage—say sympathetic or detailed coverage of a group's point of view. This is essentially what Harvey Molotch and Marilyn Lester do in their analysis of news coverage of the Santa Barbara oil spill.[7] They find that federal officials and oil business repesentatives were more successful in promoting their points of view in newspapers outside of Santa Barbara than were conservationists and other local interests. Molotch and Lester offer this as evidence for differential access to the nonlocal media. They assume that relatively little coverage of conservationist activities is proof of little access of conservationists to the media outside of California.

However, from the data provided, we cannot know exactly why coverage patterns developed as they did. We can neither be certain of the different access seeking behavior on the part of various actors nor of the media's response. It would not be surprising to learn that local organizations exerted much greater effort in interacting with the local newspaper than they did with the national press. Moreover, the national media system is complex. Blockage or inadvertent neglect of particular stories could have occurred at any of a number of points and for any number of reasons. Without additional information on the access-seeking behavior of local conservationists and the response of various news people, it is impossible to assess the ability of conservationists to get a hearing with the nonlocal press.

Group access to the press can be thought of as an interaction between some group member and some media person, in which the former talks and the latter listens. There are four questions one might ask about these interactions in an effort to understand the media's role in interest group politics. What form do group-media interactions take? Under what conditions do various forms occur? What are their consequences for the amount and type of coverage? And, finally, what are the consequences of these interactions and the resulting coverage for group strength and group success?

Answers to these questions are far from settled. One type of group that has been the subject of study is the resource-poor or disadvantaged group.[8] These groups often resort to confrontation as a tactic, and the mass media are seen as particularly crucial to such groups as they try to reach and influence public officials. Below, we consider what we know about confrontation as a media tactic for resource-poor groups.

RESOURCE-POOR GROUPS AND THE PRESS: MYTHS AND REALITIES

There seems to be widespread agreement that confrontation leads to media coverage, but some doubts about the long-term desirability and effectiveness of this coverage for group goals. The conventional wisdom goes something like this. Resource-poor groups are driven to confrontation out of frustration because nothing else works—conventional modes of participation are either not open to them or judged to be useless. Group leaders do not have access to the media and cannot communicate with public officials through other traditional channels, such as overlapping memberships and social contacts. They lack resources to bargain positively.[9] Consequently, they engage in confrontation—peaceful or violent—and the media then cover their activities, though not necessarily their viewpoints. The media stories emphasize the facts of the confrontation as an event— the number of people participating and the incidence of arrests or damage—and generally ignore the underlying issues leading to the confrontation in the first place. Meanwhile, coverage of the event may turn off potential members who do not want to be arrested or hit over the head, and may turn off important third party allies as well. In the long run, this weakens the group and its challenge fails.[10]

While this description sounds plausible, parts of it do not hold up under empirical investigation. First, do groups engage in confrontation out of frustration at being blocked through legitimate means? This is a common theme underlying much legal opinion deaing with First Amendment cases. There is an assumed relationship between the stability of the system and adequate opportunity to participate and communicate within the system. For example, Judge Irving Kaufman wrote the following in an opinion for the U.S. Court of Appeals for the 2nd Circuit:

> We should in these times be mindful that to the extent we secure le-
> gitimate and orderly access to means of communication for all views,
> we create conditions in which there is no incentive to resort to more
> disruptive conduct.[11]

There is an assumption that communication is enough to avoid disorder. But what group leaders want are advantages and recognition and acceptance. Talk will not always keep them quiet. Nor is a lack of talk always what precipitates action.

My own study of four protest groups operating in Boston during the late 1960s and early 1970s leads me to doubt that a lack of access to and coverage in the media causes or encourages most protest activity.[12] The usual circumstance is for group leaders to assume media disinterest without ever approaching reporters to discuss their concerns in the first place, and to be quite surprised when group activities—even their protest activities—are covered. When organizers from outside the community come in with previous media experience, sometimes events are staged with the media in mind, but not so much because the organizers cannot capture media attention in other ways. Rather, they stage protests because they want to convey messages about group vitality and strength that they think are better conveyed through protest action. The major point is that most protest activity is not an outburst by people who have tried to reach the media and failed, but usually a planned activity intended to produce certain results.

This perspective on the relationship between protest activity and media access meshes nicely with Peter Eisinger's conclusions about protest activity and the local political sytem more generally. Eisinger describes protest as the "product of a cost-benefit calculation."[13] He finds that groups engage in protest not so much out of frustration with an unresponsive community leadership, but rather out of impatience with communities that are, in fact, moderately responsive.

William Gamson's study of 53 challenge groups focuses on violence, not peaceful protest, but his conclusions are similar. He finds that violent action is not the result of frustration with legitimate political means but rather "an instrumental act, aimed at furthering the purposes of the group that uses it when they have some reason to think it will help their cause."[14] Violence, for Gamson's groups, grows out of impatience and confidence, not frustration or desperation.

The second step in the conventional wisdom—that confrontation, especially violent confrontation, receives media attention—is better supported by empirical work. Fedler's study of groups in Minneapolis, referred to above, shows that minority groups received coverage when they engaged in confrontation and seldom otherwise. Studies of the validity of newspaper data in conflict research also demonstrate that the intensity of a conflict is a good predictor of coverage.[15]

By now it is also commonly accepted that media coverage of confrontations does not include a thorough discussion of motivations and issues. This was one major conclusion of the Kerner Commission's study of media coverage during the ghetto disorders of the 1960s—that the media failed to report thoroughly on causes and consequences of civil disorders, that instead they emphasized official (and often inaccurate) reports about property damage, personal injury and deaths.[16] Fedler's work in Minneapolis and Barron's more impressionistic report also support this conclusion. So, while the first point in the conventional wisdom is not well supported by recent research results, this second point is.

The final step in the conventional argument is once again questionable—that the use of confrontation hurts the group's chances of success in the long run either by discouraging potential members and supporters or by damaging the group's image as a legitimate participant in the political system. Gamson finds that "unruly groups," those which initiate violence or strikes, are relatively successful as compared with those that do not. The most impressive difference, however, is not between those who do and do not use confrontation. Instead, it is between those who initiate confrontation and those who are subjected to official violence, arrest or harassment. Those groups that initiate confrontation are substantially more successful in gaining advantages and in gaining acceptance than are those on the receiving end of official violence.[17] The interesting thing about this for media research is that each of these situations is on face equally newsworthy and likely to receive media attention. Yet, one is related to success and the other is not. This raises questions of whether the media's treatment of violence and conflict has much to do with eventual outcomes, and if so, in what way. It also suggests the need for research on media treatment of confrontation users and recipients.

Jenkins and Perrow's study of two farm workers' movements challenges a specific piece of the conventional wisdom—that publicity of failures hurts group maintenance and eventual group success.[18] They describe how the United Farm Workers were able to motivate important third party allies on their behalf even in the face of press reports on their unsuccessful strikes and official violence against UFW members. This case is particularly interesting because of its atypical properties. Jenkins and Perrow report that the farm workers were able to capture the attention of the eastern press, particularly the *New York Times,* even though their challenge occurred mainly in California. The UFW actually received more press coverage in the *New York Times* than in the *Los Angeles Times.*[19] This can be contrasted with the more usual pattern of coverage illustrated in Molotch and Lester's study of the Santa Barbara oil spill;[20] typically, the geographical proximity of an event or issue is a powerful predictor of amount of news coverage. It is possible that the UFW was somehow able to target its media messages cleanly to separate targets, something unusual for most interest groups. They may have reached the eastern liberal elite—their third party allies—with certain messages and their potential members in California with quite different messages. If so, they could have overcome the problems of appealing to four separate constituencies simultaneously that Lipsky describes in his study of rent strikes in New York City.[21] Jenkins and Perrow's study invites further investigation into the UFW-media relationships that developed over time as well as the relevant audience characteristics for the various media involved. Like Gamson's work, it raises more questions than it answers about the consequences of using confrontation as a media tactic. It is clear that much work remains to be done before we can adequately assess this third part of the conventional wisdom.

It is important to remember that all of these studies begin with groups that receive at least some media attention. But many groups may not surface to make their challenge visible. The media could help such groups gain enough visibility to enter public discussion if the media engaged in some form of active outreach, seeking out different points of view. A number of scholars have argued that because of the media's profit motive[22] or because of their identification with the prevailing values in the local community[23] or because of various organizational routines,[24] outreach is unlikely to happen. The last section of this paper discusses several factors that affect a group's ability to gain access to the media.

GAINING ACCESS TO THE PRESS: THE MEDIA ORGANIZATION

Gaining access to the media depends on a number of things, including properties of the media organization, the interest group and the situation.[25] The focus in this chapter is on the media organization and specifically on the organization of daily newspapers. However, many of these points are relevant to the electronic media as well.

Besides the obvious organizational characteristics, such as amounts of space, deadlines and staff size, which limit newspaper capabilities, there are interesting properties of newspaper organizations with special importance for the access of nongovernmental groups. The effort here is to highlight certain newspaper procedures that affect media outputs adversely from the perspective of those concerned about the access of groups with widely varying viewpoints.

In order to minimize uncertainty, newspapers operate according to certain standard operating procedures that define the conventions of news reporting. One important set of procedures is the allocation of newspaper resources. The allocations of two resources—space and personnel—are important in determining who has access to the metropolitan newspaper. Each is discussed below. Rather than the immediate decisions about allocating a reporter to a specific story, what are discussed are the broader allocational decisions that affect whether or not newspaper personnel is likely to become aware of a story in the first place.

Space is allocated in advance to various sections of the newspaper—columns, features, national news, local news and so forth. The column is an important case. By making some space regularly available that must be filled by someone writing on a specific topic, the newspaper can encourage that columnist to initiate contacts with potential sources. A columnist also provides a visible newspaper contact for sources who want to generate stories on that topic. On most newspapers, it is more common to have columns written by beat reporters or columnists assigned to some institution, such as the state house, than to have columns that intentionally reach into the community. However, this is a matter for management and columnists to decide. If columns are assigned to cover specific subpopulations—women, minorities, elderly and so forth—with space regularly allotted and restricted to that particular subject, it can ease access problems for interest groups active on behalf of those population segments.

A second type of space allocation made in advance is for international, national, metropolitan and local news. Certain pages, or certain numbers of stories per page, are set aside for news about different geographic areas. Newspapers more committed to international and national news are less likely to pay attention to groups with strictly local concerns. Since newly emerging groups are usually local in nature, at least in the beginning, they may experience real access difficulties until they can define their challenge in broader geographical terms.

Space is not the only newspaper resource allocated. So is staff. News personnel is assigned to write columns, cover beats, report general assignments and develop specialties. Virtually every newspaper maintains a general assignment staff, considered by most to be the backbone of the news operation. General assignment reporters are assigned to stories by editors. They may develop expertise over time in one or several broad areas of reporting, but in general they are expected to be able to cover anything and everything. While most specialists and beat reporters maintain their own files of information, general assignment reporters cannot, due to the wide variety of information they might need at any time. Usually they have to write about fairly unfamiliar news items on short notice. They rely on memory, on newspaper morgues and on the information they can gather on any particular day. Moreover, general assignment reporters are expected to describe an event accurately; they are not usually expected or encouraged to explain it. As a result of the demands of their assignment and the expectations of their editors, general assignment reporters may miss a newly emerging group. If they notice the group, they may judge it as insignificant when compared with other better-known participants in the event. And if they judge the group significant enough to be mentioned, general assignment reporters may describe group activities but neglect group messages. The procedures used by general assignment reporters make it unlikely that interest group views will be heard and understood in any detail except as they can be expressed through some event or action.

A second type of allocation of newspaper personnel is to the beat. Most newspapers establish beats at institutions where news is expected to break regularly: the police station, courthouse, city hall or state house. Beat reporters are responsible for news of their institution and the prominent officials who are based there. Because official sources are more likely than interest group sources to have beat reporters assigned to them, they are more able to gain the attention of beat reporters.

The conventions of news gathering on the beat rely heavily on press releases, meetings and press conferences. Official sources maintain extensive public relations staffs for the purpose of generating positive publicity and directing attention where officials want it directed. For example, a governor's public relations staff makes certain that there is an abundance of state house news. The problem for the state house reporter is to sift through all the possibilities and choose the most important news items. The bulk of the news items comes from officials and tends to serve their interests. It adopts their definition of the situation or problem and works within that framework. For interest groups to receive the attention of state house reporters, they have to break through this routine.

Furthermore, as beat reporters work with the same officials and other beat reporters day after day, they often adopt official perspectives on problems and write for each other. They can form a close-knit club in which only the members are assumed to understand what is happening and to appreciate a good story. This phenomenon has been mentioned in many studies and is usually referred to as absorption or parochialism.[26]

Finally, many beat stories concern events that are scheduled in advance. The predictability of such "continuing news" allows reporters to manage their work and to plan their time.[27] Reporters can anticipate how and when a story will develop. For example, if a suit is brought in court, reporters covering the story know in advance the various steps in the judicial process and roughly when they are likely to occur. If unscheduled news erupts, they can cover it and still know where to pick up the pieces on the continuing story. In contrast, the evolution of a social movement is not usually predictable. Protest groups may not be around tomorrow. If they are, no one can predict what they will be doing or where they will be doing it. Consequently, their efforts may not be treated as a continuing story. This places them at a disadvantage in capturing the attention of news personnel, since reporters do not plan ahead to fit them into their schedules. This is particularly serious for beat reporters on beats with so much prescheduled news that their schedules have little flexibility left.

The implications of the beat system for outsiders trying to reach government can be stated simply. Beat reporters rarely attend to non-institutional groups. The obvious exception occurs when these groups intrude themselves on some beat activity, such as appearing at a committee meeting or a public hearing. But continuing attention requires continuing intrusion, and that is expensive and often impossible. Beat reporters generate considerable news copy, regularly accounting for a large portion of the space available in the newspaper. However, in their stories, they demonstrate an overwhelming concern with political maneuvering on the beat and a strong official perspective on social problems, neither of which eases access for nongovernmental groups.

In contrast, a strong system of specialists assigned to report on trends, developments, problems and conflicts within a particular issue area can facilitate interactions with nonofficial sources. Specialists are not necessarily fixated on certain institutions or official sources, but are rather expected to produce some number of articles per week on an issue area such as education, housing, poverty or the environment. Of course, a strong specialist system is no guarantee that interest groups will receive attention. Medical specialists may be expected to cover hospital and medical school news; if the specialist goes on to cover the problems of health care delivery for the poor, it is usually because the individual reporter chooses to do so or because a particular editor pushes a reporter in that direction.

As with beats, specialties that are expected to last for some time and that encourage frequent interaction between reporter and group leaders can produce absorption and parochialism. Over time, reporters tend to redefine their "significant others" from people in the newsroom in general to other specialists or to sources. If these sources are the leaders of interest groups, it can result in access and sympathetic and informed coverage for these groups and their activities.

Different specialists define their jobs differently and follow different procedures in generating and collecting news. Some work in ways to benefit interest groups. Others do not. What the specialist system does is provide an opportunity for in-depth reporting from a nongovernmental and noninstitutional perspective—an opportunity not usually available to the beat or general assignment reporter.

Thus the decisions that newspaper management makes about allocations of space and personnel are non-neutral in their effects. Traditional allocation decisions that emphasize general assignment, beat reporting and columns about institutions may exclude community views to a degree unexpected and unintended by media management. In contrast, an emphasis on columns dealing with specific population segments and on specialties dealing with community issues can reverse the usual tilt in favor of official government views toward a more varied and balanced news product.

SUMMARY

Different people writing about access to the media have very different things in mind. Some are explaining the amounts of coverage received, some the types of coverage and some the nature of the interactions that develop between interest groups and media personnel. Each is an important piece in the larger puzzle of the role of the media in interest group politics. The perspective emphasized here is of access as a hearing in which groups express their points of view to reporters and compete for what is essentially a scarce resource, media coverage. It is important that we understand the terms of this competition.

As recent research on confrontation demonstrates, some of our common notions about the media are more myth than reality. Opening the media to many points of view will probably not reduce the levels and frequency of confrontation unless it also produces group acceptance and some shift in advantages. And merely covering confrontation with little attention to underlying problems does not constitute access. The circumstances under which press coverage of confrontations helps groups succeed or dooms them to eventual failure are yet to be documented.

One of the prevailing beliefs that many hold about the American political system is that groups can be heard before decisions affecting the lives of their members are made. What is suggested here is that some interest group leaders can be heard from time to time when they take certain initiatives. The media can do a great deal to reach these community groups in the early stages of organization and encourage their interest in the press. Newspapers can change their allocation of space and reporters in ways that invite participation by broader segments of the community. Some media have made special efforts in this direction since the urban violence of the 1960s. Others could do a great deal more.

NOTES

[1] Probably the most complete treatment of the concept of access can be found in David B. Truman, *The Governmental Process* (New York: Alfred A. Knopf, 1964).

[2] For a more thorough discussion and specific examples, see Edie N. Goldenberg, *Making the Papers* (Lexington, Mass.: Lexington Books, 1975).

[3] Roger W. Cobb and Charles D. Elder suggest that "for an item or an issue to acquire public recognition, its supporters must have either access to the mass media or the resources necessary to reach people." See *Participation in American Politics: The Dynamics of Agenda-Building* (Boston: Allyn and Bacon, Inc., 1972), p. 86. The literature on media effects on issue salience is growing vast. Much of it is summarized in Lee B. Becker, Maxwell E. McCombs and Jack M. McLeod, "The Development of Political Cognitions," in Steven H. Chaffee, ed., *Political Communication* (Beverly Hills: Sage, 1975), pp. 21–63.

[4] The Commission on Freedom of the Press (Hutchins Commission), *A Free and Responsible Press* (Chicago: The University of Chicago Press, 1947).

[5] Truman, *op. cit.*, pp. 264–65, assumes that access is an intermediate objective of all political interest groups. For a discussion of the conditions under which resource-poor groups seek access to the press, see Goldenberg, *op. cit.*

[6] Fred Fedler, "The Media and Minority Groups: A Study of Adequacy of Access," *Journalism Quarterly*, 50 (1973), pp. 109–17.

[7] Harvey Molotch and Marilyn Lester, "Accidental News: The Great Oil Spill as Local Occurrence and National Event," *American Journal of Sociology*, 81 (1975), pp. 235–60.

[8] Goldenberg, *op. cit.*

[9] James Q. Wilson, "The Strategy of Protest: Problems of Negro Civic Action" *Journal of Conflict Resolution*, 5 (September 1961), pp. 291–303; Michael Lipsky, *Protest in City Politics* (Chicago: Rand McNally, 1970).

[10] See Lipsky, *op. cit.*, for a discussion of the difficulty groups face in reaching different audiences and the problems this creates for long-term success.

[11] As quoted in Jerome A. Barron, *Freedom of the Press for Whom? The Right of Access to Mass Media* (Bloomington, Indiana: Indiana University Press, 1973), p. 98. Barron cites others in this same vein. See pp. 97, 107, 124–25 for other examples.

[12] Goldenberg, *op. cit.*

[13] Peter K. Eisinger, "The Conditions of Protest Behavior in American Cities," *American Political Science Review*, 67 (March 1973), pp. 11–28.

[14] William Gamson, *The Strategy of Social Protest* (Homewood, Illinois: Dorsey, 1975), p. 81.

[15] David Snyder and William R. Kelly, "Conflict Intensity, Media Sensitivity and the Validity of Newspaper Data," *American Sociological Review*, 42 (February 1977), pp. 105–23; also see M. Herbert Danzger, "Validating Conflict Data," *American Sociological Review*, 40 (October 1975), pp. 570–84.

[16] National Advisory Commission on Civil Disorders (Kerner Commission), *Report of the National Advisory Commission on Civil Disorders* (New York: Bantam Books, Inc., 1968), pp. 362–89.

[17] Gamson, *op. cit.*, pp. 79–87.

[18] J. Craig Jenkins and Charles Perrow, "Insurgency of the Powerless: Farm Worker Movements (1946–1972)," *American Sociological Review*, 42 (April 1977), pp. 249–68.

[19]*Ibid.,* pp. 253–54.

[20] Molotch and Lester, *op. cit.,* pp. 242–43.

[21] Lipsky, *op. cit.,* pp. 163–84.

[22] David R. Bowers, "A Report on Activity by Publishers in Directing Newsroom Decisions," *Journalism Quarterly* (Spring 1967), pp. 44–49.

[23] Warren Breed, "Mass Communication and Sociocultural Integration," *Social Forces,* 37 (1958), pp. 109–16.

[24] Goldenberg, *op. cit.*

[25] Each of these is discussed in some detail for resource-poor groups seeking access to the metropolitan press in Goldenberg, *op. cit.* Much of the following discussion is drawn from pp. 57–88.

[26] See, for example, William L. Rivers, *The Opinionmakers* (Boston: Beacon Press, 1965), pp. 23, 193–94; and Leon V. Sigal, *Reporters and Officials* (Lexington, Mass.: D. C. Heath and Co., 1973), pp. 37–64.

[27] Gaye Tuchman, "Making News by Doing Work: Routinizing the Unexpected," *American Journal of Sociology,* 79 (1973), pp. 110–31.

V

Access to the Media: Balancing Feminism and the First Amendment

by MARYANN YODELIS SMITH

University of Wisconsin—Madison

THE AUGUST, 1977, report of the U.S. Commission on Civil Rights focused on two issues: "The extent to which local broadcasters are making employment opportunities equally available to women and minorities, and the ways in which minorities and women are portrayed on television programs.[1] Although there has been improvement in these areas in the last two decades, the Commission said the data:

> . . . document very specifically the extent to which minorities and women—particularly minority women of each of the groups studied—continue to be under-represented on local station work forces and to be almost totally excluded from decision-making and important professional positions at those stations. Furthermore, minorities and women—again, particularly minority women—are under-represented on network dramatic television programs and on net-

work news. When they do appear they are frequently seen in token
or stereotyped roles.[2]

Women and minorities in communication generally lack power and
adequate pay, but not put-downs. Women and minorities, however,
throughout society share such problems and feminists specifically are
banding together to change media practices that they believe are unfair to women and minorities in communication, as well as to women
and minorities generally.

Such media challenges necessarily involve the question of First
Amendment rights. There are perhaps two basic philosophical frame-
works supporting the idea of free expression. The traditional approach is that free expression is a personal right. A more recent view
is that First Amendment freedoms are a social right.[3] In this conception, free speech and press must be balanced against other concerns
of government and society: education of the young, good order, protection. Women and minorities challenging current media practices,
while demanding the social good of access to the media by minorities,
must be particularly careful not to trample on the First Amendment
rights of the media and of the general public. The balance between
the First Amendment rights of the public the media serve and the
First Amendment rights of the media is delicate, but not impossible.

This research, then, focuses on two questions: (1) Are there
major areas in which the goals of women and minorities have tended
to encroach on the First Amendment rights of communicators? and
(2) What appear to be the most fruitful ways for women and minorities to insure fair treatment by and access to the media without eroding the First Amendment rights of another social group?

After describing the inherent tension between the right of a free
press and the right of access to the media, the study will outline the
limited right of access to the print media. Next, the essay will review
challenges to broadcast license renewal and challenges to broadcasters
under the fairness doctrine. Because of the similarities of access problems of women and minorities, cases from both areas will be utilized
interchangeably. Access to cable, however, is excluded from the discussion, since the existence of broad access rights in cable offers little
basis for extending those rights to other media.

First Amendment Foundations

First Amendment philosophy had its roots in the relatively liberal
thinking of the seventeenth century. Political theorists like John
Stuart Mill emphasized the rational person's ability to make self-

government decisions. For Mill and others, a prerequisite for intelligent decision-making was full knowledge collected from unrestricted debate on all sides of a question. In Mill's free marketplace of ideas, truth ultimately surfaces.[4] Freedom of expression is based on the person's need to participate in self-government.

Thomas I. Emerson isolates four major values protected by the concept of free expression for society. He writes that a system of free expression assures individual self-fulfillment, helps attain truth, secures participation by individuals in social (including political) decision-making and maintains the balance between stability and change in society.[5] Recognizing the creative tension between the individual's good and society's welfare, Emerson argues that only disruptive action arising from a conflict of opinions can be regulated by government. He says this interpretation of the First Amendment rests upon "the general proposition that expression must be free and unrestrained, that the state may not seek to achieve other social objectives through control of expression, and that the attainment of such objectives can and must be secured through regulation of action."[6]

Many interpretations of the First Amendment, like Emerson's, are based on the concept of a free marketplace of ideas. Justice Oliver Wendell Holmes summarized:

> But when men have realized that time has upset many fighting faiths, they may come to believe even more than they believe the very foundations of the own conduct that the ultimate good desired is better reached by free trade in ideas—that the best test of truth is the power of thought to get itself accepted in the competition of the market, and that truth is the only ground upon which their wishes can safely be carried out.[7]

On the other hand, this free marketplace of ideas has been called a romantic illusion in view of the media conglomerates of the 1960s and 1970s. One access proponent, Jerome Barron, argues that the media's opinion-making function rests in the hands of a few who are not accountable to the public. He contends that there must be a right of access because participatory democracy demands openness and diversity rather than the "myth of cultural and ethnic homogeneity continuously depicted in American cultural broadcasting."[8] Barron's solution to under-representation of minority views in the media is mass participation in the media implemented by government. Although the U.S. Supreme Court recognizes the need for minority access to media, in general, it has not viewed the right of access as consonant with the First Amendment.

RIGHT TO REPLY REJECTED

A major opportunity for recognition of the right of access presented itself in *Miami Herald Publishing Company v. Tornillo.*[9] The case involved the constitutionality of Florida's right-to-reply statute,[10] which, if upheld, would have insured that at least candidates for political office would have access to print media. As counsel for Tornillo, Barron told the U.S. Supreme Court in oral argument that the Florida statute requiring newspapers to print replies by candidates for public office to editorial criticism enhanced freedom of expression. Barron said that the law furthered the goals of the First Amendment by promoting uninhibited debate on public issues in the press.[11] On appeal from the Florida courts, the U.S. Supreme Court held the statute violative of the First Amendment.[12] Chief Justice Burger noted the sensitivity with which the Court views governmental tampering with the press and suggested that governmental coercion "at once brings about a confrontation with the express provisions of the First Amendment and the judicial gloss on that amendment developed over the years."[13]

Professor Barron's access thesis was handicapped by a sturdy line of federal cases expressing general reluctance to mandate enforced access to the press, and the oral argument in *Tornillo* made it clear that the U.S. Supreme Court agreed. Justice Marshall inquired of Barron: "What's the difference between the state saying we shall require you to publish something and saying we shall not permit you to publish something?"[14] Marshall suggested either form of print regulation was an impermissible incursion on First Amendment guarantees.

Dictum from the recent landmark decision, *Columbia Broadcasting System, Inc. v. Democratic National Committee,*[15] which upheld the right of broadcasters to refuse political editorials, apparently carried much weight with the justices. The plurality opinion in that case noted:

> The power of a privately owned newspaper to advance its own political, social, and economic views is bounded by only two factors: first, the acceptance of a sufficient number of readers—and hence advertisers—to assure financial success; and, second, the journalistic integrity of its editors and publishers. . . .[16]

In rejecting Tornillo's argument that the power to shape public opinion has been placed in a few hands, thereby homogenizing editorial opinion and commentary, Chief Justice Burger commented that a right-to-reply statute was an undesirable means of insuring that all individuals contribute meaningfully to the discussion of public issues. He agreed with newspaper publishers that economic hardship will follow enforcement of such a law because the statute constitutes a penalty of sorts for publishing the original critical content.[17] The Court recognized that a newspaper cannot "proceed to infinite expansion of its column space" in order to accommodate replies.[18] Further, the Court pointed out that a candidate's reply to a critical editorial might preempt information considered more desirable for the public good by the editor.[19] But more importantly, Chief Justice Burger said the Florida statute would have a chilling effect on publishers' First Amendment rights. Editors, he said, "might well conclude that the safe course is to avoid controversy and that, under the operation of the Florida statute, political and electoral coverage would be blunted or reduced. . . ."[20]

Even though the Justices did not find the reply statute consonant with the First Amendment, they gave a sympathetic hearing to access proponents. Chief Justice Burger noted:

> The elimination of competing newspapers in most of our large cities, and the concentration of control of media that results from the only newspaper being owned by the same interests which own a television station and a radio station, are important components of this trend toward concentration of control of outlets to inform the public. The result of these vast changes has been to place in a few hands the power to inform the American people and shape public opinion. . . .[21]

Nevertheless, the Court did not find that monopolistic trends justified abridging the First Amendment. It seems, however, inaccurate to postulate that some form of access never will emerge. Though rejecting a right of access enforced by government coercion, the Court implied, for example, that if some "consensual" method was devised, the access concept would be acceptable.[22] Burger noted that such a solution already exists as the National News Council, a nongovernmental body, which examines claims of press inaccuracy.[23] Still, in general, the Supreme Court rebuffed the argument that there is need for a new First Amendment right of access to the press, a right particularly supported by women and minorities.

THE CLASSIFIED PAGE

While treating the First Amendment rights of newspaper publishers with great sensitivity, the U.S. Supreme Court did rule that employment classified advertising under sex-segregated column head-ings violates the law. More recently, however, a Pennsylvania court rules that a newspaper may continue to publish, under a "Situations Wanted" column, advertisements by job-seekers even though the con-tents specify the race, color, religious creed, ancestry, age, sex or na-tional origin of the person placing the advertisement. Although the first of these cases, *Pittsburgh Press v. Pittsburgh Commission on Human Relations, et. al.,*[24] constituted a triumph for feminists, it was a limited decision and the principles of the case no longer can be construed as a tool for correcting other social ills in the area of commercial speech.[25] This case, as well as the second Pittsburgh Press case[26] nevertheless are well worth reviewing for their interest to women and minorities.

Pittsburgh Press I began a three-year trek to the highest court on October 9, 1969, when the National Organization for Women, Inc. (NOW) filed a complaint against the *Press* with the Pittsburgh Com-mission on Human Relations.[27] NOW said the Press violated the city ordinance prohibiting any "person" from aiding or abetting in the placement of a discriminatory advertisement.[28] After several at-tempted negotiations failed, the commission issued a cease and desist order on July 23, 1970, directing the Press to omit sexual designations in classified advertising.[29] Exhausting all lower court avenues for re-lief, the *Press* took its case to the U.S. Supreme Court and raised the First Amendment question.[30]

The briefs and oral argument recognized the socio-economic good the ordinance was intended to achieve, as well as the implica-tions for the First Amendment. Both the *Press* and the American Newspaper Publishers' Association (ANPA), *amicus curiae,* argued that the organization and format of advertising sections of a newspaper should be exempt from commercial speech regulations. The ANPA said that "it must be recognized that a newspaper's decision as to how advertising shall be displayed is as much an editorial function as its decision as to how its editorial page shall be constructed.[31] Both the *Press* and the ANPA called the lower court decisions against the *Press* another attempt to coerce publishers into the role of enforcing socio-economic legislation, thereby overstepping the bounds of the First and Fourteenth Amendments.[32]

The Commission and *amici curiae* (eight) briefs take an opposite point of view. The Commission argued that where governmental reg-ulation of speech is incidental, such speech mixed with illegal action lacks First Amendment protection.[33] The Commission charged that the *Press* actively "participated in the aiding of discrimination by itself creating the discriminatory structure."[34] Many of the briefs referred to the hearing testimony of Dr. Sandra Bem of Carnegie-Mellon University, who presented research findings that "an advertiser, by placing a want ad in the 'Male Interest' column, effectively discourages a large percentage of female applicants."[35] On balance, the Commission said that governmental interest in eliminating job discrimination against women was greater than its interest in protecting commercial speech via the First Amendment.[36]

Dismissing the due-process arguments, the U.S. Supreme Court went directly to the First Amendment question. The Court disagreed with the state judges' holding that the *Press* could not use the First Amendment to shield its employment advertising column headings from governmental regulation. The Court stressed that the First Amendment had to be balanced against other rights. However, rather than considering whether state regulation was crucial enough to overcome First Amendment claims, the Court asked whether abridgment of freedom of the press was great enough to warrant constitutional protection.[37] From this view, the Court found insignificant intrusion on the *Press's* First Amendment rights:

> . . . no suggestion is made in this case that the Pittsburgh Ordinance was passed with any purpose of muzzling or curbing the press. Nor does *Pittsburgh Press* argue that the Ordinance threatens its financial viability or impairs in any significant way its ability to publish and distribute its newspaper. . . .
>
> In a limited way, however, the Ordinance as construed does affect the makeup of the help-wanted section of the newspaper.[38]

The Court added that the advertisements were "no more than a proposal of possible employment," rather than expressions of opinion and criticism, and therefore constituted commercial speech, unprotected by the First Amendment.[39] The Court said nothing in the sex-designated column heading "dissociates the designation" from the want ad beneath it to make the placement of column headings severable from advertisements for First Amendment purposes.[40] The Court rejected protests that the Commission order constituted a prior restraint on the *Press:*

> . . . nothing in our holding allows the government at any level to forbid *Pittsburgh Press* to publish and distribute advertisements commenting on the Ordinance, the enforcement practices of the Commission, or the propriety of sex preferences in employment. Nor, *a fortiori,* does our decision authorize any restriction whatever, whether of content or layout, on stories or commentary originated by *Pittsburgh Press,* its columnists, or its contributors. On the contrary, we reaffirm unequivocally the protection afforded to editorial judgment

and to the free expression of views on these and other issues, however, controversial.[41]

On the other hand, the four dissenters[42] found a significant encroachment on the newspaper's editorial judgment in organizing the classified advertising columns. Chief Justice Burger warned that the Commission order was prior restraint.[43] Justice Douglas said even commercial matter has First Amendment protection because no law in the First Amendment means no law.[44] Justice Stewart (joined by Justice Blackmun) concluded his dissenting opinion with a ringing defense of the First Amendment:

> So far as I know, this is the first case . . . that permits a government agency to enter a composing room of a newspaper and dictate to the publisher the layout and makeup of the newspaper's pages. This is the first such case, but I fear it may not be the last. . . . After this decision, I see no reason why Government cannot force a newspaper publisher to conform in the same way in order to achieve other goals thought socially desirable. . . .
>
> Those who think the First Amendment can and should be subordinated to other socially desirable interests will hail today's decision. But I find it frightening. For I believe the constitutional guarantee of a free press is more than precatory. I believe it is a clear command that Government must never be allowed to lay its heavy editorial hand on any newspaper in this country.[45]

Thus, the Court in this one instance found for women complaining of sex-designated advertising. Nevertheless, it seems that women and minorities ought to consider carefully the minority concerns in the dissenting opinions and rethink the concept that major social goals might be a greater good than an individual editor's First Amendment rights. Even *Pittsburgh I* chips away at the theory that a free marketplace of ideas ultimately will permit women and minorities to promulgate their views. But more importantly, the U.S. Supreme Court no longer supports the commercial speech doctrine reiterated in *Pittsburgh I* that purely commercial speech has no First Amendment protection.

Giving commercial speech at least some First Amendment protection generally removes advertising as an area where women and minorities might strive to achieve their goals. For example, in *Bigelow v. Virginia*,[46] the U.S. Supreme Court overturned on First Amendment grounds the conviction of a newspaper editor for publishing an advertisement for an out-of-state abortion referral agency. The Court held that the advertisement had some First Amendment protection even though it was commercial speech and said that First Amendment interest must be balanced against the interest of the Commonwealth of Virginia in prohibiting such advertising. The Court emphasized that *Pittsburgh I* dealt with a situation where the commercial activity being advertised was illegal and the restriction on advertising was incidental to a valid limitation on economic activity.[47] Less than a year later, the Court permitted price advertising for prescription drugs by licensed Virginia pharmacists.[48] The Court said, however, that commercial speech did not carry with it the full Constitutional protection of other speech. For example, regulation of time, place and manner of advertising, of false and misleading advertising, of advertising illegal activity and of broadcast media advertising still is permissible.[49] Therefore, in *Pittsburgh II,* the Pennsylvania Court voided the cease-and-desist order against the *Press* for publishing "Situations Wanted" advertisements with specifications of the sex or race of the job-seeker. After reiterating that commercial speech does have some measure of protection, the Court noted that in *Pittsburgh II* the subject is individuals who choose to classify themselves. The Court suggested that forbidding such advertisements would not further the Commission's interest in combatting discrimination, but, indeed, might significantly impair the flow of legitimate and truthful commercial information.[50] This broadening First Amendment protection to commercial speech, coupled with the *Tornillo* decision and the courts' consistent position that media are not obligated by the First Amendment or laws of unfair competition to carry advertising they do not wish to publish,[51] generally closes the door to government-enforced access to the print media for women and minorities.

Access in Broadcasting

As noted in the discussion of *Tornillo,* there also has been a collision between advocates of a public right of access to the airwaves and the First Amendment rights of broadcasters. Although *Columbia Broadcasting System, Inc. v. Democratic National Committee*[52] was not brought by women, the case has applicability to other women's right of access cases and deserves further discussion. The DNC case in reality contracts the right of public access to the media previously construed more widely by dicta in the *Red Lion* case that indicated it was the First Amendment right of the public, not of the broadcaster, that was paramount.[53] In the CBS case, the Women's Institute for Freedom of the Press took the access position:

According to the First Amendment, freedom of the press belongs to everyone, not just those who own the media. We must find ways for all Amerians to have equal access to their fellow citizens—so people can get to know each other as they really are, not as interpreted by others, and so the public can hear and benefit from the contributions of all of us.[54]

The U.S. Supreme Court, however, disagreed.

The courts took three years to deal with the issue of public access to the media in the DNC case. In May, 1970, the Democratic National Committee requested the Federal Communications Commission (FCC) for a declaratory ruling that "a broadcaster may not, as a general policy, refuse to sell time to responsible entities, such as the DNC, for the solicitation of funds, and for comment on public issues."[55] The committee claimed it needed to buy radio, television and national network time to implement a nationwide effort to appeal for funds and to publicize views of the Democratic Party, the loyal opposition, on current issues. The FCC said such a ruling would be contrary to the regulatory scheme of the electronic media under the 1934 Communications Act. The FCC did, however, uphold the DNC's right to solicit funds. The U.S. Court of Appeals (D.C.) reversed the FCC, holding that a "flat ban on paid public issue announcements is in violation of the First Amendment, at least when other sorts of paid announcements are accepted."[56]

The U.S. Supreme Court, accepting the case on a *writ of certiorari,* reversed the decision on the grounds that broadcast frequencies are a scarce resource and that the long history of legislative and administrative decisions has developed a regulatory system that best serves First Amendment rights of viewers and broadcasters.[57] Chief Justice Burger wrote that "the public interest standard of the Communications Act of 1934, which invites reference to First Amendment principles, does not require broadcasters to accept editorial advertisements."[58] He reiterated the *Red Lion* majority opinion that the broadcast media pose unique problems not present in other First Amendment cases because of the physical limitations of the medium. Frequencies, Justice Burger said, must be rationed and all who wish to use the airwaves cannot be accommodated. He said, "It is idle to posit an unabridgable First Amendment right to broadcast comparable to the right of every individual to speak, write, or publish."[59] The Court further rejected the argument that the licensee discriminates by accepting commercial advertisements while refusing editorial advertisements. Rather, the majority opinion accepted the fairness doctrine as the prescription for broadcasters.[60] Justice Burger did, however, write that "conceivably at some future date Congress or the Commission—or the broadcasters—may devise some kind of limited right of access that is both practicable and desirable."[61] The opinion probably should be construed as affording the FCC more time to achieve a satisfactory balance between the First Amendment rights of the broadcaster and the access rights of the public. The press and the courts have been dealing with this balance in areas of broadcasting other than the paid political editorial question.

Access Skirting the First Amendment

If one accepts the view that further erosion of the First Amendment, exemplified by *Pittsburgh I,* is not desirable and that the courts will not require broadcasters to accept paid public issue announcements, there still are avenues available to women and minorities that do not erode traditional First Amendment concepts. These are: (1) challenges to license renewal and construction permits, (2) challenges to staging practice and (3) challenges brought under the fairness doctrine. Although these issues do not deal with the access question squarely, these means of challenging broadcasters have permitted minority groups some measure of voicing their own ideas in the media. Rather than deal with a universe of cases in each of the three areas, only illustrative cases are discussed.

Citizen-licensee interaction is based on representation and participation. In a sense, the airwaves are loaned to broadcasters on the condition that the power is used for the "public interest, convenience and necessity."[62] However, the courts clearly have placed the authority to make programming decisions with the broadcasters. Because broadcasters have not been elected to represent the public, the FCC has mechanisms to make broadcasters at least indirectly accountable to their constituents. Some citizen groups, seeking representation and participation, have interpreted the U.S. Supreme Court's endorsement of the concept as a license to obtain specific programming concessions from some broadcasters.[63] Because of their encroachment on the broadcaster's programming responsibilities, some citizen groups have appeared insensitive to the First Amendment.

On the other hand, some scholars have suggested that citizen attempts to interfere with programming are not outrageous in view of social attitudes toward women and minorities and in view of the FCC's tendency to respect always the broadcaster's discretion. Political scientist and feminist, Jo Freeman, wrote that this need for citizen initiative and broadcaster goodwill reveals a pluralist assumption about the structure of the politial system. She said, "Government is not prepared to enforce its own law; rather, it must wait until organized interests force it to do so."[64]

The solution, then, is finding the delicate point of balance where broadcasters can be made accountable as public fiduciaries without giving up their First Amendment rights. The most effective strategy to insure diversity of views in broadcast programming has been for citizen groups to negotiate with broadcasters. Rather than describe the terms of such citizen-licensee agreements, this study will review the First Amendment balancing employed by the courts in the three areas of license renewal, staging protests and fairness doctrine cases.

License Renewal

Discriminatory employment practices of broadcasters might be better challenged at license-renewal time, at the application for a construction permit or when a license is transferred. This is based on the assumption that women and minorities must be employed in greater numbers in the media to insure that the diversity of opinion on the air includes those of women and minorities. FCC rules and regulations provide that broadcast licensees afford equal opportunity in employment and that no licensee discriminate on the basis of sex.[65] Each licensee required to establish and continue a positive program to assure equal employment opportunity. Stations violating the FCC rules thereby violate state and federal non-discrimination laws, particularly Title VII of the 1964 Civil Rights Act. Such violations raise questions about the broadcaster's ability to operate in the public interest. License-renewal challenges by citizen groups, of course, do not preclude lawsuits brought by women and minority employees under federal, state and local equal-opportunity statutes. However, such laws are outside the scope of this discussion.

Although the FCC requires a showing of affirmative action by broadcasters, citizen challenges to license renewal generally require a more extensive documentation of discrimination. For example, the FCC granted seven Florida stations regular renewals in 1974; they appeared unresolved toward eight stations (although these were directed to follow affirmative action guidelines) and required 24 licensees owning over 30 stations to submit a list of local minority and women's organizations, agencies, community groups, schools and colleges, with which the licensee will maintain systematic communication each which there is a job opening. The 24 licensees also were expected to submit with annual employment reports a detailed statement of affirmative action steps taken when job openings occurred. License renewals were contingent upon fulfilling the requirements. The FCC commented that affirmative action requires licensees to make positive efforts to recruit minorities and women, but it does not require reverse discrimination, i.e.. offering positions to unqualified minorities rather than to qualified non-minorities.[66] However, broadcasters need only show a good faith effort toward compliance. Only stations with fewer than six employees are exempt.[67]

On the other hand, challenging groups must make a more extensive case to prove discrimination. For example, courts have held that a showing of disparity between the percentage of minority group members in the community and the percentage employed by the station does not establish a *prima facie* case for denying license renewal when the broadcaster has a policy of minority recruitment and of placing minorities in responsible positions. Statistical evidence of an extremely low rate of minority employment might make a *prima facie* case, however.[68] In a Massachusetts incident, the Commission said an examination of statistical data regarding minority and female employment by Massachusetts television stations showed that such employment fell within a "zone of reasonableness" when those figures were compared with appropriate population statistics.[69] Appropriate statistics were used for minorities, but not for women. The FCC added that several of the Massachusetts stations employ few, if any, full-time employees in the upper four job categories (officials and managers, professionals, technicians and sales workers) and ordered such stations to increase efforts to employ women and minorities in those positions.[70] Perhaps because the FCC seems unfairly to place a heavy burden of proof on women nd minority complainants,[71] the Washington, D.C., Appeals Court admonished the Commission. The Court suggested that the FCC policy of making challenging groups show specific instances of discrimination might be unrealistic in view of the limited resources of those groups and in view of the unavailability of discovery procedures until a case is designated for hearing. The Court concluded: "But if minorities are not given *some* means for developing the reasons for statistical disparities, hearings may have to be required based on such disparities alone, in order to provide the tools of discovery."[72]

In early 1977, license-renewal cases indicate more sharply that the courts are willing to prod the FCC and broadcasters to fulfill their obligations to citizens. For example, discovery procedures and full hearings have been mandated in license-renewal cases. The U.S. Court of Appeals (D.C.) upheld the request of the Bilingual Bicultural

Coalition for discovery procedures when the coalition challenged a license renewal with claims that the licensee's employment practices were discriminatory.[73] The FCC can renew licenses without a hearing, but the Court noted that this often leaves major issues only superficially resolved and that the public interest might not be adequately considered. The court added that renewal, even when coupled with routine station monitoring, could merely postpone and perpetuate discriminatory conditions antithetical to the public interest, rather than remedy specific deficiencies that might have been revealed clearly in a discovery process. In this case, the coalition accompanied its objections to license renewal with written interrogatories requesting precise data from the licensee relating to employment practices. The station ignored the request because the FCC rules did not provide for such interrogatories and gave information "emphasizing experience subsequent to the filing of the petition, and coupled this with expressions of good intent for the future."[74] The Court suggested that the FCC revise its procedures to include the discovery process so that the Commission can support its commitment to eliminate discrimination in employment by fact-finding efforts. The Court agreed that license-renewal hearings are last resorts, but suggested that the FCC must not decide to forego hearings without full knowledge of the facts through prehearing discovery processes. The Court said:

> We hold that before the Commission makes a determination in a particular license renewal case to grant renewal without a hearing, it has a duty to afford a petitioner opposing renewal with claims of discriminatory practices by the station in question . . . an opportunity to probe the station's initial representation in response to the petition by making a record which includes more than the filings of the parties and statistical information available in Commission records. It must afford those challenging renewal a reasonable opportunity for prehearing discovery through appropriate interrogatories. Of course, if the interrogatories are irrelevant or overly burdensome the Commission through its hearing examiners may impose appropriate limitations.[75]

Two other 1977 cases in the same court provide more guidelines on when the FCC will be required to hold a full license-renewal hearing. When the Black Broadcasting Coalition challenged a license renewal for alleged racial discrimination in employment and inadequate affirmative action,[76] the FCC did not require a hearing. The Court remanded the case to the FCC for a full hearing, noting that the broadcaster's performance had been outside the "zone of reasonableness." The Court said:

For example, the Commission found it significant that by 1975 the percentage of blacks employed at WTVR-TV had risen to 13.7 percent and at WTVR-AM-FM to 9.5 percent. It found these figures to be within the zone of reasonableness, even though the increase at WTVR-AM-FM was due in part to attrition of white employees rather than new hiring of black employees. The past history of 1.5 percent or less black employment during the license period in an area where blacks constitute about one-fourth of the local work force went wholly unexplored. Further, allegations of overt discrimination in hiring and firing remained uncontested and unsatisfied.[77]

The Court further noted that affirmative action means more than a passive acceptance of referrals and frowned on the broadcaster's failure to establish a training program to qualify blacks and women for more significant jobs at the station.[78] The trend of cases clearly indicates that citizen groups must present specific factual data if those groups expect support from the courts in license-renewal challenges. Such challenges are within the framework of First Amendment freedoms. However, the courts also have made clear that they will not require the FCC to hold a license-renewal hearing if the citizens' petition does not contain "specific allegations of fact sufficient to show . . . that a grant of the application would be *prima facie* inconsistent with (the public interest)."[79] If specific allegations have not been made, the FCC may refuse to hold a hearing after concisely stating the reasons. The courts will not review such action unless it appears arbitrary, capricious or unreasonable.[80] The economics of providing full and specific fact allegations, of course, may be prohibitive to some citizen groups; however, that is beyond the scope of this discussion.[81]

Staging Practices

Although citizen challenges to broadcaster staging practices probably have eliminated the practice, FCC staging policy remains only a slap on the wrist of the offending licensee. Women and minority groups found staging practices particularly offensive because of the misleading portrayal of them as a group. Public hearings on such practices were held by the Subcommittee on Investigations of the House Committee on Interstate and Foreign Commerce. Because of allegations of staging in ABC's Seattle police wives story and in the CBS documentary, "Powder Puffs and Handcuffs," the subcommittee testimony was referred to the FCC.[82] Commission policy can be summarized:

. . . if the allegations of staging, supported by intrinsic evidence, simply involve news employees of the station, we will, in appropriate

cases . . . inquire into the matter, but unless our investigation reveals involvement of the licensee or its management there will be no
hazard to the station's licensed status. Such improper actions by employees without the knowledge of the licensee may raise questions as
to whether the licensee is adequately supervising its employees, but
normally will not raise an issue as to the licensee's character qualifications.[83]

This should not, however, preclude women and minority groups
from protesting and investigating staging practices when they occur.

Fairness Doctrine

Finally, women and minorities have challenged broadcasters
under the fairness doctrine, but with little success. Women's groups
have charged broadcasters with presenting a biased point of view of
the women's role in society and with ridiculing or withholding information on the women's rights movement.[84] The fairness doctrine
requires that the licensee, to operate a station in the public interest,
should (1) devote a reasonable amount of time to programming controversial issues of public importance and (2) cover these issues
fairly.[85] Broadcasters are required to afford only reasonable opportunity for discussion of contrasting views. The broadcaster not only
chooses the controversial issues to be covered, but has the discretion
to make good-faith judgments on programming and presenting the
issues. The licensee, however, cannot wait for offers to present opposing views, but must affirmatively encourage and implement presentations of opposing views, even though it is at the station's expense
when sponsors are unavailable.[86] Generally, women's challenges
under the fairness doctrine have been unsuccessful because the complaints lacked specific charges.[87] The complainant is required to state
the issue, the time of the broadcasts, and to prove that in overall
programming, the broadcaster failed to present opposing views.
Again, the economic burden of providing documented and sophisticated research data may be too heavy for complainants to bear.

Even when large, organized groups like NOW have presented
statistics, descriptions of offensive presentations, and excerpts from
programming allegedly violating the fairness doctrine, the courts have
not been willing to substitute their judgment for that of the FCC in
denying the citizen claims.[88] Generally, all parties have agreed that a
woman's role in society is a controversial issue of public importance.[89]
The debate occurs over the judgment of whether the broadcaster
made a conscious effort to present opposing views. In a 1977 fairness
case brought by NOW, the Court upheld the FCC view that con-

troversial issues may be raised by entertainment programming and advertisements, but:

> if the ad bears only a tenuous relationship to (an ongoing public) debate, or one drawn by unnecessary inference the fairness doctrine would clearly not be applicable.[90]

The Commission in a fairness report stated that the usual product commercial cannot be said to inform the public on any side of a controversial issue of public importance.[91] In the NOW case, the Court upheld the FCC practice of seeking general balance in overall programming, leaving specific programming determination to the broadcaster. "The Commission approach under the fairness doctrine of looking at the overall programming and of not requiring any scientific or mathematical equality in the balance afforded contrasting views is rooted in the stated policy of the Commission, and has been repeatedly approved by this Court."[92]

Although fairness-doctrine challenges and staging challenges are permissible as long as the complainant remains sensitive to the editorial discretion given the broadcaster by the First Amendment, these tools have not proved effective for women and minorities trying to achieve social change. It seems, however, that well-documented license-renewal challenges have been more effective tools by comparison.

CONCLUSIONS

In summary, then, women's groups and minorities must recognize the tenuous balance between seeking social reform and encroaching on the First Amendment. The U.S. Supreme Court has, for all practical purposes, found that imposed access to the print media by government enforcement is inconsistent with the First Amendment. Although *Pittsburgh I* showed that on occasion there are a few areas of expression where reforms may be sought, the chink chiseled from First Amendment protection proves hardly worth the victory. Women and minorities, it seems, can best reach their social goals by insisting on non-discrimination in employment practices through enforcement of existing state and federal equal-opportunity laws, and then depending on the increased number of women and minority employees and management personnel to change the nature of communications. Also, because courts have accepted the physical limitations theory of government broadcast regulation, there appears to be more opportunity for women and minorities to challenge discriminatory words and broadcast practices without encroaching further on broadcasters' First Amendment freedoms. However, there has been no direct right of access established by the courts to the airwaves for citizens, with the exception of the limited access in cable-casting. The courts have emphasized the broadcaster's discretion to edit and to make programming decisions. The courts further have refused to compel broadcasters to carry advertisements of political or public interest commentary. Stringent burdens of proof are placed on citizens complaining to the FCC about broadcasters' practices. A vast array of statistical data is needed by challenging groups. Perhaps the greatest value of such challenges, however, even if the citizens lose the case in court because of First Amendment considerations, is the accompanying public pressure on the broadcaster to modify or change discriminatory practices. If the pattern of broadcast regulation changes substantially, to the extent of abolishing the fairness doctrine, for example, it seems that the emphasis on broadcaster discretion will increase and the effectiveness of citizen complaints will decrease.

Although the recommendation has been made to women and minority groups that the best arena in which to achieve non-discriminatory practices in the communications media may be that of public opinion, care must be taken by complaining citizens to insure respect for First Amendment freedoms. Citizen agreements, reached with broadcasters, and even with the print media, in negotiations outside the courtroom, are a fruitful way to achieve change so long as the First Amendment is cherished. As Judge Bazelon warned with a quotation from Lord Devlin:

> If freedom of the press . . . perishes, it will not be by sudden death.
> . . . It will be a long time dying from a debilitating disease caused by
> a series of erosive measures, each of which, if examined singly,
> would have a good deal to be said for it.[93]

NOTES

The author is grateful to Suzanne Pingree for her continued support during the research and to Kim Rhodes Smith and Lisa Smith for whom this work was completed.

[1] U.S. Commission on Civil Rights, *Window Dressing on the Set: Women and Minorities in Television* (Washington, D.C., 1977), p. 3.

[2] *Ibid.*

[3] Miami Herald Publishing Co. v. Tornillo, 418 U.S. 241, 94 S.Ct. 2831, 41 L.Ed.2d 730 (1974).

[4] John Stuart Mill, *On Liberty* (Northbrook, Illinois: AHM Publishing Corporation, 1947).

[5] *Toward a General Theory of the First Amendment* (New York: Vintage Books, 1966), p. 3.

[6] *Ibid.*, p. 115.

[7] Abrams v. United States, 250 U.S. 616, 40 S.Ct. 17 (1919).

[8] *Freedom of the Press for Whom?* (Bloomington: Indiana University Press, 1973), p. 300.

[9] *Ibid.*

[10] Florida Statutes Annotated, section 104.38 (1973).

[11] 42 U.S.L.W. 3590 (April 23, 1974).

[12] *Miami Herald*, pp. 256–57.

[13] *Ibid.*, p. 254.

[14] 27 U.S.L.W. 3590 (April 23, 1974).

[15] 412 U.S. 94, 93 S.Ct. 2080, 36 L.Ed.2d 772 (1973).

[16] CBS, p. 117.

[17] *Miami Herald*, p. 256.

[18] *Ibid.*, p. 257.

[19] *Ibid.*, p. 258.

[20] *Ibid.* The *Herald* contended the fear of lawsuits, as well as the possibility of obscene or defamatory replies submitted for publication by candidates, might keep conscientious editors from printing anything about impending elections.

[21] *Ibid.*, pp. 249–50.

[22] *Ibid.*, p. 254.

[23] *Ibid.*, note 19. The National News Council is an independent and voluntary body concerned with fairness in the press. It was created in 1973 to provide a neutral forum for examining claims of press inaccuracy. Its enforcement power is merely public opinion, however. Nevertheless, it also should be noted that the courts have found that the pressure exerted on broadcasters by the National Association of Broadcasters to maintain family viewing hours on television violates the First Amendment. *Writers Guild of America, West, Inc. v. FCC* and *Tandem Productions v. CBS*, U.S. District Court, C.D. Calif. #CV 75-3641-F, CV75-3710-F, November, 1976.

[24] 413 U.S. 376, 93 S.Ct. 2553, 37 L.Ed.2d 669 (1973). Hereinafter called *Pitts-*

burgh I. The author acknowledges the research assistance of Barbara Lonnborg in obtaining copies of the briefs.

25 See *New York Times v. Commission on Human Rights* No. 541, New York Court of Appeals, February 10, 1977, where the court held the *Times'* publication of an ad that lists employment opportunities in South Africa, but did not express, directly or indirectly, discriminatory conditions of employment, does not violate New York City anti-discriminatory laws. In addition, it will be shown later that the commercial speech doctrine reiterated in Pittsburgh I was since overturned.

26*Pittsburgh Press Company v. Commonwealth of Pennsylvania, Pennsylvania Human Relations Commission,* Commonwealth Court of Pennsylvania, No. 1275 Commonwealth Docket 1976, July 21, 1977.

27 Pittsburgh Commission on Human Relations brief (Commission Brief), 1972, p. 2.

28 Pittsburgh Human Relations Ordinance #75, Section 8(j) as amended by Ordinance #395.

29 Commission Brief, pp. 2–6.

30 Appeal of *Pittsburgh Press,* FEP cases 558 (Allegheny County, Pa., 1971), aff'd Pittsburgh Press Employment Advertising Discrimination Appeal, 4 Pa. Comm. 448 (1972) modified the order to allow sex-designated headings for advertisers not covered by the ordinance and for advertisers who obtained bona fide occupational exemption from the Commission. *Pittsburgh Press v. Pittsburgh Commission on Human Relations,* Superior Court of Pennsylvania (1972), denied the Press appeal with one justice voting to consider the First Amendment issue.

Earlier state and federal court cases did not reach the First Amendment issue. See *Brush v. San Francisco Newspaper Printing Co.,* 315 F. Supp. 577 (D.C.N.D. Calif., 1970), aff'd 469 F.2d 89 (CA9, 1972). The statute is 42 U.S.C. 2000 e-3 (b). Also, *Greenfield v. Field Enterprises,* 4 E.P.D. Par. 7763, 5930 (N.D. Ill., 1972); *Morrow v. Mississippi Publishers,* 5 E.P.D. Par. 8415, 7045 (S.D.Miss., 1972); *National Organization for Women v. Gannett,* 338 N.Y.S.2d 570, 40 A.D.2d 107 (1972); *NOW v. Buffalo Courier-Express,* 337 N.Y.S.2d 608, 71 Miss.2d 917 (1972).

31 American Newspaper Publishers' Association Brief, *Pittsburgh Press I,* pp. 2, 15, hereinafter ANPA Brief.

32 ANPA Brief, p. 7.

33 Commission Brief, pp. 26–27.

34*Ibid.,* p. 31.

35*Ibid.,* p. 5; ACLU Brief, pp. 9–10, note 10.

36 Commission Brief, p. 32.

37 Pittsburgh I, p. 382.

38*Ibid.,* p. 383.

39*Ibid.,* p. 385; the holding was reversed in later cases, notes 47, 48.

40*Ibid.,* p. 388.

41*Ibid.,* p. 391.

42 Burger, Blackmun, Stewart, Douglas.

43 Pittsburgh I, p. 395.

[44] *Ibid.*, p. 398.

[45] *Ibid.*, pp. 402–3. Douglas also joined. Blackmun did not subscribe to the portion beginning "After the decision. . . ."

[46] 421 U.S. 809 (1975).

[47] *Ibid.*

[48] Virginia State Board of Pharmacy v. Virginia Citizens Consumer Council, Inc., 425 U.S. 748, 96 S.Ct. 1817 (1976).

[49] *Ibid.*

[50] *Pittsburgh II,* p. 11.

[51] See *Mississippi Gay Alliance v. Goudelock,* 536 F.2d 1073 (5th Cir. 1976) cert. den. 52 L.Ed.2d 377 (1977); Person v. New York Post Corp., 427 F.Supp. 1297, 2 Med. L.Rptr. 1666 (E.D.N.Y. 1977).

[52] CBS, p. 2080.

[53] *Red Lion Broadcasting Co. v. FCC,* 395 U.S. 367, 89 S.Ct.1794, 23 L.Ed.2d 371 (1969).

[54] *Media Report to Women,* January 1, 1974, p. 1.

[55] In Re Democratic National Committee, Washington, D.C., Request for a Declaratory Ruling Concerning Access to Time on Broadcast Stations, 25 FCC2d 216 (1970).

[56] *DNC v. FCC,* 450 F.2d 646 (D.C.Cir. 1971), 146 U.S.App.D.C. 256 (1971).

[57] DNC S.Ct. at 2101. The case was joined by Business Executives for Vietnam Peace, ABC, and *Washington Post-Newsweek* Stations. In Re Business Executive Move for Vietnam Peace was 25 FCC2d 242.

[58] DNC, p. 2080.

[59] *Ibid.*, p. 2086.

[60] *Ibid.*, pp. 2000–2100.

[61] *Ibid.*

[62] 47 U.S.C. section 151 et. seq.; also *Red Lion,* 367, where the court said: "There is nothing in the First Amendment which prevents the government from requiring a licensee . . . (to) conduct himself as a proxy or public fiduciary with obligations to present those views and voices which are representative of his community and which would otherwise, by necessity, be barred from the airwaves."

[63] *Office of Communications of the United Church of Christ v. FCC,* 359 F.2d 994 (D.C.Cir. 1966) gave standing only to citizen groups.

[64] "The Sexual Caste System," 5 *Valparaiso University Law Review* (1970–71), p. 204.

[65] FCC Report and Order Docket #19269, Dec. 28, 1971, effective Feb. 4, 1972, and Docket #18244; FCC Rules and Regulations, Section 73.125 (a) and Section 73.125 (b).

[66] In the Matter of Inquiry into the Employment Policies and Practices of Certain Broadcast Stations Located in Florida, FCC 74-18/07803, 29 RR2d 285, adopted January 3, 1974.

[67] FCC modification of rules to stations with fewer than 11 employees struck down by U.S. Ct. of Appeals (2nd Cir. N.Y.) as arbitrary and capricious. See Les Brown, "FCC Equal Employment Rules Voided," *New York Times,* August 9, 1977, 59M.

[68]*Stone v. FCC,* 151 U.S. App. D.C. 145, 24 RR2d 2105 (1975).

[69] In the Matter of Letter to Everett C. Parker, Director, Office of Communications, United Church of Christ, Re 1972 Massachusetts Television Stations License Renewals adopted December 19, 1973, FCC 73-1349/07394, 29 RR2d 245.

[70]*Ibid.*

[71] See, for example, In Re Application of KSAY Broadcasting and San Francisco Wireless Talking Machine Company re License to KSAY-AM San Francisco, FCC 74-161/10239, 29 RR2d 809 or in Re Application of Regents of University of California, Livermore, California, FCC 14-1907805, File No. BIPF-301, January 3, 1974, 29 RR2d 228.

[72]*Bilingual Bicultural Coalition of Mass Media v. FCC,* U.S.Ct. of Appeals, D.C., Feb. 13, 1974, 29 RR2d 745 (1974).

[73]*Bilingual Bicultural Coalition of Mass Media v. FCC,* 2 Med.Law Rptr. 1705 (1977).

[74]*Ibid.,* p. 1706.

[75]*Ibid.,* p. 1707.

[76]*Black Broadcasting Coalition v. FCC,* Roy H. Park Broadcasting of Virginia, Inc., 2 Media Law Rptr. 725 (1977).

[77]*Ibid.,* p. 1727.

[78]*Ibid.,* p. 1728–29.

[79] NOW v. FCC, 2 Media Law Rptr. 1609, 1610 (1977).

[80]*Ibid.,* Also see *Action for Children's Television v. FCC,* U.S., ABC, CBS, 2 Media Law Rptr 2120 (1977).

[81] See Joseph A. Grundfest, *Citizen Participation in Broadcast Licensing Before the FCC* (Rand Corporation, March, 1976).

[82] Seven other staging incidents not involving women also were investigated. Staging occurs when broadcasters use actors and/or request participants to repeat an event for the benefit of the cameras, yet lead the viewing audience to believe that the event was spontaneous. See Hearings of Subcommittee on Investigations of the House Committee on Interstate and Foreign Commerce, May 18, 1972.

[83]*CBS v. FCC,* 20 FCC2d 150 (1969).

[84] For example, refer to transcripts of press conference of Whitney Adams, September 1, 1972, on day of filing complaint against WRC-TV, a Washington, D.C., NBC station.

[85] See Report on Editorializing by Broadcast Licensees, 13 FÇC 1246; Fairness Doctrine Primer, 29 Fed. Reg. 10415 (1964); Legislative History of the Fairness Doctrine, Staff Study for House Interstate and Foreign Commerce Committee, 90th Congress, 2d Session, 89–742 (1968); Fairness Doctrine, Staff Report for Senate Subcommittee on Communications, 90th Congress, 2d Session (1968).

[86] The personal attack and political editorial rules require more specific behavioral compliance.

[87] For example, see complaint of *Georgia Franklin v. WKNX,* Los Angeles, Dec. 22, 1972, June 31, 1972 and staff ruling, Jan. 17, 1973; complaint of *V.E. Minnennette v. WJBO,* Baton Rouge, La., Feb. 5, 1973, staff ruling; and

Harry Britton v. WTTG, WTOP-TV, Washington, D.C., March 16, 1973 staff ruling. More recent cases have followed the same pattern.

[88] NOW, p. 1613.

[89] See Marc A. Franklin, *Mass Media Law* (Mineola, N.Y.: Foundation Press, 1977), p. 753, for a good explanation.

[90] NOW, p. 1617; also Fairness Report, 48 FCC2d 23.

[91] *Ibid.,* p. 26.

[92] NOW, p. 1618.

[93] *Yale Broadcasting Co. v. FCC,* Case #71-1780 (D.C. Circuit), March 28, 1973.

VI

Women, Media Access and Social Control

By GERTRUDE JOCH ROBINSON
McGill University

AT THE END of a decade during which female journalists and lay groups have increasingly protested the scanty representation of women in media jobs as well as the scanty attention paid to women in North American media coverage, it is time to ponder and assess what the shouting is all about. This chapter will place the problems of media access into a larger social framework. It will view the portrayal of women's issues not as an isolated phenomenon but as related to the aims of the femininst movement and the social control functions of the mass media in American society.

"Female media access" is an ambiguous concept that has been studied from at least three basic perspectives. These may be roughly designated as political, sociological and symbolic. Political studies of "access" are concerned with media-source relationships. They analyze strategies for organizing and gaining media attention,[1] developing symbiotic relationships with reporters[2] or analyzing connections between media and power centers.

Another way to study "access" is to look at the ability of qualified women to enter the work area of their choice. Here sociologists like Epstein and others have discovered that women's entry into the work arena is hindered by sex role definitions and socialization.[3] These channel the majority of females into a small number of low prestige occupations. Bowman[4] and my own study of the journalism profession in the United States and Canada furthermore indicate that within media, women are a minority of 20% and are segregated into the less prestigious specialities and at the lowest ranks in the organizational hierarchy.[5]

In contrast, considerably less attention has been paid to the symbolic dimension of the mass media, as cultivators of a particular type of outlook and understanding. Viewing them merely in terms of ownership or distribution obliterates their human dimension, their role in creating and reflecting how a community of people come to talk and think about themselves. Linguists and anthropologists have highlighted the crucial role of language in the conceptualization of everyday life. They observe that language enables us to interpret and organize the world we experience through our senses and in this way it provides structure and meaning to what would otherwise be a jumble of impressions. In doing this, language however also limits what speakers in a particular community pay attention to and define as "real." The most widely shared of these definitions are made public through our mass media.

Media output studies have primarily focused on static categories, such as the prevalent portrayals of women's roles in television comedies, advertising, children's programming and daytime serials.[6] Very little systematic attention has been lavished on linking outputs to social changes and on dealing with the broader question of how the daily public-discussion agenda selects and defines women's issues.

To shed light on this issue, we shall define "access" in symbolic terms as "a person or group's ability to be attended to (gain mention) in the daily public-discussion agenda." Such an investigation must concern itself not only with media outputs or performances in isolation. It must inquire as well into the processes by which outputs are related to those who are being portrayed and to those who are doing the portraying. This chapter will therefore not only illuminate the conceptual mechanisms involved in public-meaning creation, but the ways in which access affects the symbolic processes of legitimation. Three interrelated questions therefore require answers: (1) what are the processes involved in public meaning creation, (2) how are women's issues presented and (3) how has changing access affected portrayals and legitimations throughout the past decade?

Our culturological approach makes various assumptions. To begin with, it assumes that the media, as institutional and symbolic realities, their audience and those who are daily described, are all part of a single interacting whole, in which no element can be said to determine the other. Public definition-making, furthermore, is an institutional process occurring in a particular time and place. Newspapers and radio stations develop persistence, because the people working there share similar interpretations about common goals and functions. Consequently, the media content produced is influenced by what journalists perceive to be commonly accepted ways of viewing and defining reality.

Furthermore, we are aware that public conceptualization involves various groups of people with different expectations. Among these are journalists with their news production values, various women's groups wishing to change public descriptions of female issues and the general public, as audience, sharing a one-dimensional conception of female and male roles.

Finally, we believe that the output or pictures of women's affairs produced for North American consumption are not isolated phenomena. They are instead governed by underlying social values that are widely expressed in other verbal and non-verbal dimensions of our culture. The way in which women's activities and their work outside the home are portrayed thus has something to do with the collective definitions and evaluations of women's changing role.

The Mechanisms of Public-Meaning Creation

A variety of writers have noted that the news is not one reporter's view of an event, but a social product molded by a variety of organizational and professional demands.[7] As a result, the news-making process from the techniques of reporting through the technology of publishing sets a distinguishing stamp on the overall product that appears daily in the North American commercially sponsored media. Some of the most obvious and widely documented values shaping the news-gathering process are objectivity, timeliness and responsiveness to visibility. "Objectivity," contrary to popular belief, does not refer to the truthfulness of media interpretation, but demands merely impartiality of coverage, which is stylistically supplied by quoting two opposing sources. "Visibility" plays a role in the selection of commentators, preference being given to top-position holders and experts. "Timeliness," in turn, refers to the characteristics of the public-discussion agenda itself and to what the media through previous coverage have attended to. With respect to all of these general criteria, women are at a disadvantage as compared to men. The probability that a woman will be selected for expert comment, now holds a visible decision-making position or has figured in the news before is less than that of her male counterpart in our society. How much less is not yet exactly known.

To these general news values must be added another: "news judgment." This consists of the relatively unrecognized and unintended biases that arise in the course of evaluating a potential story's emphasis, prominence and inclusion in the daily public agenda. Breed[8] and others have described the way in which news judgment is learned by the new recruit through reading his own paper—observing the blue penciling of his editor, paying attention to headlining and becoming familiar with the publisher's personal stands on local issues. "News judgment" is thus a "consensual agreement derived from common occupational experiences, standardized criteria and practices transmitted from the more to the less experienced, from the higher to the lower ranking."[9]

That the widely shared expectations of the professional journalist tend to standardize popular perceptions and definitions of social situations was first noted by Lippmann 50 years ago. He described social stereotyping as a process whereby "in the great blooming, buzzing confusion of the outer world, we pick out what our culture has already defined for us and we tend to perceive that which we have picked out in the form stereotyped for us by our culture."[10] The editor utilizes this social stereotyping as a framework for dealing with the headline-harried choices he must make about every bulletin crossing his desk. "Without standardization, without stereotypes, without routine judgments, without fairly ruthless disregard of subtlety, the editors would soon die of excitement," Roshco notes.[11]

What are some of these social stereotypes molding women's news? By what criteria are women's issues judged newsworthy? Unfortunately, there are few specific answers to this question, except Gena Corea's, which is based on a survey of editorial opinion. Corea found that women are considered newsworthy if they meet one of the following criteria: they have an important husband, have beauty, were victimized, have political significance, are performers in the arts or athletics, show ability as homemakers or hold "first woman" status—for example, "first female Little League shortstop."[12] These seven cri-

teria may be classed into three groups: neutral, stereotyped and victimized, and it may be assumed that they affect selection and play of
women's issues in different ways.

The institutional and ideological setting in which the production
of women's news occurs on the North American continent suggest a
number of testable predictions. In the light of our assumption that
news values are embedded in a larger structure of social stereotypes
about women, we must hypothesize that women, as a more home-
bound and less important group, will also receive less frequent and
less long coverage on the daily public-discussion agenda. Furthermore, what is selected will appear in a lesser position, be this in a spe-
cialized section of the newspaper or lower in the broadcast presentation sequence.

Even the "neutral" news values that are applicable to both men
and women, such as political significance, being a performer or a first
person of some kind, will work against the selection of women-related
items. The reason for this is that they apply to a potentially smaller
pool of women than men. In our society, it is not women but men
who carry high community rank, are in leadership positions or enjoy
expert status. As a result, stories with female news makers will not appear as frequently as stories with male news makers and if they do,
women news makers will most likely be of lesser status.

The sex stereotypical news criteria, on the other hand, which
include having an important husband, beauty or homemaker abilities,
have another effect. They do not necessarily inhibit access to the
public-discussion agenda, but they will tend to funnel reporting about
women into the less prestigious human interest and personality sections. Such reporting deals with people in their private rather than
their public capacities and thus reinforces the prevailing opinion that
women engage in the "lesser" pursuits. Finally, the criterion of "vic-
timization" will most likely increase the probability of sensational selection and thus inhibit the use of scarce newspaper space for the
reporting of other areas of women's lives. Some indication for this
comes from a NOW report of New York's *Daily News* coverage.[13]

MONTREAL PILOT STUDY:
SEX, NEWS VALUES AND THE PORTRAYAL OF WOMENS' ISSUES

To test the various hypotheses about the effects of news values on
the availability and content of women's news, Montreal's public CBC
(Canadian Broadcasting Corporation) and private CTV (Canadian
Television Network) news broadcasts were content-analyzed. To mini-

TABLE 6-1

Newsmakers by Sex, Subject Matter and Status

Subject Matter	No. of Items With Male Newsmakers	Status of Newsmaker*			No. of Items with Female Newsmakers	Status of Newsmaker		
		High	Medium	Low		High	Medium	Low
Hard News government, business finance, police, justice, labor, urban affairs, agriculture	94 (61%)	73	11	10	10 (33%)	4	2	4
Human Interest, personalities, and Disasters	53 (37%)	39	6	8	13 (63%)	10	-	3
Typical Women's Content**	4	1	2	1	6	4	1	1
Sports and Weather	2	1	1	-	1	-	1	1
TOTALS	153	114 (75%)	20 (13%)	19 (12%)	30	18 (60%)	3 (10%)	9 (30%)

* Status: High: holding top position in business or government, being public personality; Medium: person with organizational affiliation Low: private individual without organizational affiliation

** Typical women's content as defined by Guenin.

mize event bias, we created a composite week's sample from the first two weeks in March, 1977, including both hour-long 6 and 11 o'clock news reports. To come to grips with the ambiguity of the term "women's issues" three types of women's news were investigated: events in which women participated as news makers, special types of subject matter assumed to be of particular interest to a female audience (categories derived from women's sections in newspapers) and events reported by female media personnel.

Television news broadcasts were used for this pilot study for two reasons: they prepare a shortened public-discussion agenda, which is easier to analyze, but include the most relevant stories from CP's (Canadian Press) record, which originates from newspaper contributions.[14] Because the study was narrowly conceived and carried out over a short time span, the figures to be presented should be viewed as indicative only. We cannot assess their absolute merit until larger projects with better samples have been undertaken.

To begin with, the number, frequency and positioning of women-related items are indeed small, short and lower in the lineup. The Montreal study found that only 5 out of 24 items were generally devoted to women news makers, women-related subject matter or items reported by females. These items took up approximately 8 of the 45 minutes, and constituted 16% of the program time. Such a figure is fairly close to the 20% newshole space devoted to women's issues in the lifestyles sections of selected U.S. daily papers.[15] As to positioning, our study found that women-related stories were on the average 13th out of 24 in the line-up, which is just below the halfway mark. In this position, presentations are of course also shorter, averaging less than a minute as compared to 2 to 2½ minutes for the top stories.

To check the influence of the three "neutral" news values on selection, we classified women-related items by a news maker's sex, subject matter and status. This material is summarized in Table 6–1. It indicates that out of 469 items in the composite week, only 39% had single-sex news makers, the majority were about mixed groups of people. Among these items there are 153 with male (85%) and only 30 (15%) with female news makers. These figures corroborate the more restrictive screening effect of the neutral criteria, e.g., political significance, performer and first-person status on the selection of women-related items. Though these figures are merely indicative, they harmonize with a newspaper study of female-name mentions. Here the national and internationally oriented *New York Times* had only 17% female news makers in its issue, as against the *Mt. Holyoke Transcript,* a local paper, with five times as many mentions.[16] It thus seems that women are more likely to be selected as news makers on the local than on the national and international scenes.

The negative relationship between sex and status is also corroborated by Table 6–1. Though the majority of both types of news makers are of high status, proportionally more males (75%) than females (60%) hold top positions in business or government or are public personalities. Significantly, also twice as many female (30%) as male (12%) news makers are low-status or without affiliation. They represent people in the street, housewives, or secretaries interviewed about their private opinions.

In addition to the generally lower status of female news makers, they are also seen to be engaged in less important activities. Of all women news makers, 63% are involved in human interest, disasters and women's affairs, which are not frequently rated top of the news. Examples of this are Margaret Trudeau's interview on her clothes preferences, women concerned with school-bus fatalities or complaining about the lack of health clinics for the aged. In contrast, virtually the same percentage of male news makers (61%) are involved in government, business, finance, labor or justice matters.

The relationship of sex to subject matter is further explored in Table 6–2, which graphically indicates that the sex stereotypical news values including an important husband, beauty or homemaker status favor a selection of female-related items into the less important categories. Importance in this case is judged by the quantity and positioning of the different content items. Column 1 indicates that 58% of the total items are hard-news oriented, with government, business/finance and police/justice on top in the lineup, according to our Montreal study. Human interest items placed second with 30% and women's content ran a distant third with 10% of the total items presented throughout the composite week. Yet, the female-related items, a mere 107 out of 469, have quite different content priorities. Instead of mirroring the hard-news bias of the total sample, Column 2 indicates that female-related items fall overwhelmingly (64%) into the human interest and women's content categories.

Moreover, it appears that the sex of the reporter is also correlated with subject matter. Here, Column 4 indicates that where 59% of the hard-news items are covered by males, women are double as likely (20% versus 8%) to cover women's content. Though this is not a startling finding in the light of what we know about newspaper practices, it is interesting to note that it occurs as well in broadcasting,

TABLE 6-2

Distribution of Female Related Subject Matter by Category and Sex of Reporter

Subject Matter	No. of Items		Reporter's Sex	
	Total	Female Related*	Male	Female
Hard News				
government	105	13	95	10
business and finance	82	3	74	8
police and justice	49	7	40	9
labor	17	2	13	4
urban affairs	14	8	8	6
agriculture	3	1	2	1
	270 (58%)	33 (30%)	232 (59%)	38 (49%)
Human Interest				
human interest	88	3	76	12
personalities	41	10	35	6
disasters	13	10	9	4
	142 (30%)	23 (21%)	119 (30%)	23 (30%)
Women's Content				
medicine and health	16	16	10	6
education	13	13	6	7
ecology	6	6	6	0
organiz. & assoc.	5	5	4	1
women's employment and rights	3	3	2	1
social welfare	2	2	2	0
consumer affairs	1	1	1	0
	46 (10%)	46 (43%)	31 (8%)	15 (20%)
weather	6	3	5	1
sports	5	2	5	0
	11 (2%)	5 (6%)	10 (2%)	1 (1%)
TOTALS	469	107	392(100)	77(100)

* A "female related" item is one which either has a female newsmaker, a female reporter or falls into women's content as defined by Guenin.

Guenin's categories include: adolescence, aging, community improvement, consumerism, economics, education, employment, equality movement, hobbies, housing, humor, legal problems, marriage, medicine, mental health, population control, single life, transport, volunteers services.

where no women's desk exists. In the Montreal study, this coincidence was explained by the fact that three of the five women on the CBC staff choose to cover beats that have traditionally been of interest to women. They are education, consumer affairs and health. The other two hold general news assignments.

This dearth of women-related content in broadcasting mirrors a finding by Guenin in print. Here, too, when newspapers update their content and switch from traditional women's to "people's" or "today" sections, they do not cover additional women-related material. Instead, traditional subject matter is replaced with stories about movies, books, theatre, travel, arts and entertainers.[18] This trend toward substituting entertainment content, when viewed in the larger context of our society's disinterest in women's issues, should prove no surprise. It is merely one more example of how difficult it is to get the media to change their reporting priorities without a more fundamental reassessment of women's roles on the part of everyone. Why this is so will be further elaborated in the next section.

What implications can we draw from this material about access of female-related material to the public-discussion agenda? There are a number of relationships between sex, presentation and content in the mass media that require summary. To begin with, the study has shown that few female-related news items are presented in the daily public-discussion agenda. Out of an average of 24 items, 5 or barely one quarter are women-related in any way. This means that they are either presented by, or contain a female news maker, or are about subject matter supposed to interest women. Moreover, the women-related items were found halfway down the daily discussion agenda in about thirteenth place. Considering that the importance of a news item depends on its place in the lineup, the scarcity and positioning of women-related items shows that they are undervalued and will therefore face disproportionate access difficulties.

Access of women-related news to the public-discussion agenda is further exacerbated by the low status of female media personnel. Female reporters, it appears, never cover a lead story and are more likely to be associated with the reporting of women's content areas. Whether the fact that female reporters tend to cover the less important events is a result of choice, inclination or organizational processes is as yet impossible to tell. We do know however that sex-stereotyped professions such as journalism, wherein 80% of the personnel are men, tend to funnel minorities into restricted work areas, such as the women's desk. These then become devalued because they do not provide the requisite experience for promotion up the professional or managerial tracks. This suggests that younger female reporters must be encouraged to branch out of the stereotypical beats in both print and broadcasting to obtain greater visibility and prestige as well as the relevant experience necessary for eventual promotion.

A final factor making the access of female news to the public-discussion agenda more difficult emerges from the context in which news makers are mentioned and from their social status. Here, not only the prevalence of male over female news makers, but the fact that the former are overwhelmingly (61%) associated with politics and economics tends to work in favor of their selection for reportage. Female news makers, on the other hand, are primarily associated with human interest situations (63%), which are generally judged less important. The differential status of the two classes of news makers subtly corroborates these differences in prestige. Four-fifths of all male news makers are represented as heads of government or business organizations engaged in activities affecting the public welfare, and only 12% are portrayed as private citizens. Among female news makers, not quite two-thirds are public personalities—who are however engaged in private activities—and the final third are low-status housewives and people in the street. Such a consistent differentiation of news makers subtly reinforces the prevailing image of women and women's affairs as occurring in a privatized realm, while the more powerful men are concerned with the running of government and society.

FEMINISTS AND THE MEDIA

While the previous two sections have dealt with the process of public image-making and their effect on women's issues, we will here place women's access struggle into a larger historical perspective and look at feminist-media relations. A number of writers both past and present have pointed out that the media in any society have at least four general functions, among them to purvey basic societal values that tend to support existing viewpoints and institutional structures. This tendency to harmonize differences and mold a common outlook is as often as not achieved by not reporting what are perceived as deviant outlooks rather than according them mention in the public-discussion agenda.[19] By filtering out the new, the controversial, the challenging, conflict is dampened and change is slowed.

TABLE 6-3

Feminist-Media Relations 1966–1977

Time Period	Access	Mode of Portrayal	Social Control (legitimation)
1st Period 1966-69 movement getting organized	none	none	Blackout no legitimation
2nd Period 1970-72 "press blitz" and reluctance to grant interviews	restricted through reportage of "safe" reporters	sensationalist	Cooptation legitimization by sanitizing or excommunication
3rd Period 1973-77 established and financially viable feminist organizations	routinized less restrictive	selective subject matter less prestigeous mode	Trivialization legitimation of more aims and norms

Though we still lack detailed information, Table 6-3 assembles historical information relating to feminist-media relations between 1966 and 1977. Much of this evidence comes from Jo Freeman's[20] in-depth study of women's liberation as well as a handful of other works, including various NOW analyses and the *Media Report to Women*. Our analysis was restricted to the 11 years since 1966 because they coincide with the founding of the new feminist organizations that are spearheading the second feminist revolution on this continent. This evidence indicates that the media have gone through at least three phases in their coverage of feminism, which are in turn related to growth stages in the feminist movement and to the types of access that were available at the time.

According to Freeman, the three years between 1966 and 1969 saw both the "older" and the "younger" branches of the movement organize themselves. The older and more professionally oriented women, many of whom had worked on President Kennedy's or states' commissions on the status of women, got started earlier. They founded the National Organization of Women (NOW) under Betty Friedan in 1966. The organization's aims were initially very broad— equal professional and economic participation for women in American life. Task Forces were set up in 1968 to study discrimination against women in employment, education, religion, the family and politics, as well as in the portrayal of women in the mass media.[21] The younger group, many of whom had participated in the civil-rights and campus unrests, did not set up an umbrella organization, but got together in a variety of small groups. According to Shulamith Firestone, these can be subdivided into two branches, the politicos and the feminists. The first, with leftist political loyalties, formed caucuses within the Young Socialist Movement, Weatherman, and such, emphasizing the overthrow of capitalism, while the radical feminists established consciousness-raising groups across the continent to change women's self-images and aspirations.[22]

Through this initial period, NOW's organization failed to substantially increase its membership because it focused its effort at the national level. The more grass-roots-trained younger branches, on the other hand, began to proliferate steadily and probably had a few thousand members. Members of both NOW and the "younger" branch became active in 1969. They picketed media institutions like the *New York Times,* were part of WITCH hexes on Wall Street and sponsored the second Miss America protest at Atlantic City in early September. The latter featured a "freedom trash can" into which bras, girdles, false eyelashes and other instruments of female oppression were tossed.[23] These events were duly covered by the underground press, like New York's *Village Voice,* but the movement was otherwise virtually ignored by the established media.

In spite of these activities, access to the public-discussion agenda did not exist. In Los Angeles, one of the centers of organizing activities, coverage of feminism was a mere 19 units in the 12 months between July 1968 and 1969. Similar findings occurred for a sample of British papers a year later.[24] Such social control through news blackout does not prove that a conspiracy of silence existed, or that the media followed a calculated strategy. It does indicate, however, that the media mirrored the prevailing opinion that women and their activities did not merit public attention.

With increasing numbers and organization power, women's groups did burst on the public consciousness between January and

March of 1970, when the ubiquitous "press blitz" occurred. At this point, virtually every major publisher and network in the country did a story on women's liberation, and a fad was launched. No one knows why the media responded virtually at the same time, but evidence suggests that the New York head offices, where personnel know each other, were responding to the same sequence of public events. This blitz, which for the first time brought feminist aims and activities before the public, increased both NOW and liberation groups' participation by as much as 50%.[25]

At this point then, social control through silence gave way to limited access and an attempt at cooptation. Social control through cooptation used two approaches: it ridiculed and excommunicated the deviant values professed by some of the more extreme feminist and lesbian groups, while it tried to play down legitimate demands through judicious "sanitation." Cooptation in the broadcast media took the form of sensationalist ridicule of the symbolic "bra-burners" (an event that never occurred), while it soft-pedaled the serious challenges posed by employment, pay and status inequalities. Such portrayal tended to place women's issues beyond the realm of fair and accurate reportage and elicited radical countermoves. Leaders of the "younger" and more radical groups decided to bar male reporters and to accept no more interviews unless adequate broadcast time with no interruptions and editing was guaranteed.

There were two reasons behind the refusal to speak to male reporters. First, it was designed to force the media to hire more women and to give females a chance at reportage otherwise denied them. In addition, it guaranteed better coverage because of the common sex-related experiences of all women socialized in America. The refusal to speak to male reporters had two curious benefits according to Freeman. Initially, at least, it increased the number of movement stories, because these became a challenge. Moreover, it served as an attention-getting device, sensitizing women reading stories that ridiculed feminism to read between the lines.[26]

In the case of magazine and newspaper coverage, cooptation took the form of "sanitizing." This was achieved either by having a male reporter rewrite the article or by assigning it to a "safe" female. The first happened to Susan Brandy's story on the movement, commissioned by *Playboy*. The second was the method chosen by *Time* in its first in-depth study. Mrs. Brine, the wife of a *Time* executive, was judged to be "level-headed about the whole business of women's liberation." Yet she too turned out a personal conversion story. Lynn Young, on the other hand, never got her interpretation into print on the grounds that it was not "objective" enough.[27] As it turned out, these stories had as much effect on the media as they did on the movement. Women writers, researchers and secretaries became conscious of their secondary role and shortly after began the *Newsweek* class action suit that set the pattern for others.[28]

A third approach to feminism seems to have become prevalent after late 1972/73, when NOW graduated from a seat-of-the-pants operation and the movement was swelled by women forming groups around issues such as race, trade unionism and office work. Between 1967 and 1974, NOW went from 14 to 700 chapters, from 1,000 to 40,000 members, and increased its budget from a few thousand dollars to half a million.[29] With this expansion came a radicalization of official concerns about poverty women, sports, rape and issues not directly related to sex, like the war in Vietnam and the restructuring of sex-roles in society.[30]

Meanwhile, task forces that had been set up earlier, began to publicize their findings. The discrepancies in female media-portrayal became widely advertised and supported by such organizations as the United Methodist Women, the American Association of University Women (AAUW) and university based professionals who began to form caucuses in their associations. As a result, the National Media Taskforce of NOW filed its first petition against broadcast license renewal in 1972 and NOW's Women's Institute for Freedom of the Press organized a feminist media information exchange through its *Media Report to Women* (1973). These efforts have borne fruit in greatly increased access of a variety of women's groups to the public-discussion agenda.

Portrayal, however, as our Montreal pilot study suggests, is still restrictive and though serious coverage is now assured, it is generally couched in a less prestigious mode. Social control today is exercised through a relatively narrow selection of women's issues and through what may be called "trivialization." By belittling the social activities and contributions of women, the priority of men in North American society is implicitly upheld. The reporting of feminism and women's issues reflects this new approach both in subject matter selected and in the language used for description. Earlier sections have already documented the dearth of female-related items in the public-discussion agenda, their low rank in the lineup and the prevalence of news makers in human interest situations. It remains here to focus on trivialization resulting from the mode of description. Three mechanisms can be isolated: the use of less prestigious language, selection of less prestigious details to report and, finally, the ridicule of legitimate claims. Since the effects of these mechanisms are well known, they require only cursory illustration.

The use of less prestigious language in the reporting of situations involving women includes first-name substitution, the avoidance of professional titles and overemphasis on marital status. Miller[31] mentions that from antiquity, people have recognized the connection between naming and power. Naming conventions consequently changed over time to meet the changing interests of society. Before 1800, when women contributed to the household economy on equal terms, married women lost their last names only and were generally known by a combination of social title and first name. "Mistress Margaret" was at that time the accepted form of address.

Further devaluation occurred after 1800, as women became less visible in the public sphere through urbanization and technological change. At this point, their attachment or non-attachment to a male became the only matter worth noting. Women consequently became known as "Mrs. John Jones," advertising their married or available state. Such a change submerged not only their ability to identify themselves without reference to someone else, but women's contributions to procreation were obscured as well.

First-name substitution, as in the headline "Nixon Assures Golda Mideast Will Balance," is another instance using naming conventions to underline status distinctions. In this case, devaluation arises out of the fact that reciprocity of naming conventions is not being observed. Only the young or inferior are ordinarily called by their first names. Professional titles, moreover, are designations of prestige in most societies and thus subtly conflict with the devalued status accorded to women. No wonder the media find it difficult to apply them and that they prefer to designate a woman by her social title when reporting her actions.

The selection of less prestigious aspects for reporting is summarized by Bill Moyer, who asked: "Why does the press identify Golda Meir as a grandmother, but not Georges Pompidou as a grandfather? Why does the press talk about a female politician's hair coloring and dress style, but not the hair dye or tailor used by a Presidential candidate or Senator."[32] Much of this type of reportage, as we have seen, is a result of the sex-stereotyped news values mentioned earlier. These select and portray women in relation to their husband and family, their forms of adornment or beauty and their homemaker abilities. All of these tend to screen out a female's public achievements.

In addition, trivialization is achieved by the widely noted mecha-

nism of heaping ridicule on serious issues pertaining to women.
NOW's study of both the *New York Times* and the *Daily News* noted that
the Equal Rights Amendment, abortion and child care issues received
very little coverage or were ridiculed by these papers.[33] Headlines capture this trivialization even more succinctly as in "Women March to
War on Men and Each Other" or "McGov Woos Labor, Farmers, and
Lib Chicks." Here, another trivialization mechanism noted by Orwell
in his analysis of "Newspeak" comes into play. Abbreviating a name
subtly alters its meaning by cutting out much of the associations that
would otherwise cling to it. Such a narrowing arouses the minimum of
echoes in the speaker's mind and thus reduces the anxiety associated
with the threatening topic.[34]

ACCESS AND LEGITIMATION

The increased activities of a variety of NOW organized media
groups and others in the seventies indicate that both the "older" and
the "younger" factions of the women's movement did not view the
media access struggle merely as agitation for more accurate portrayal.
Media access, for these politically trained women, had more far-
reaching social implications—it offered a political strategy for the re-
distribution of social prestige.[35] Such political struggles, according to
Gusfield, are status struggles, which differ from class conflict in their
goals and strategies.[36]

In status struggles the strife is over the allocation of prestige
rather than the allocation of material resources. Such strife occurs
when a group makes claims to greater prestige than it has made in the
past or when the prestige accorded it is less than that expected. Both
of these conditions were at work in spurring on feminists. Freeman
notes that the "older" group expected action and respect as a result of
their public work on the Status of Women Commissions, while the
"younger" had degrading experiences in the conventions of the new
politics groups, of which they were members.[37]

Reallocation of prestige, however, is not an objective but a sub-
jective thing. It requires an alteration in the estimation of other
groups, which cannot be generated by political means alone. They are
the consequence of a much more difficult process, the rearrangement
of public perceptions. Unfortunately status conflicts are less readily
compromised than class conflicts in the American political system.
They lack institutional mechanisms for compromise. This is evidenced
by the fact that NOW and the Women's Equity Action League form a
lobby for equal rights legislation, educational, pay and tax inequali-

ties. Other feminist concerns like day care, marriage, property rights and abortion, however, lack well-defined interest groups as sponsors. The very polarization and acrimoniousness of much of the early feminist debate is a result of this lack of social mechanisms for status compromise, which then becomes fixed upon groups that are in status opposition.[38]

In spite of the fact that our typology registers only the grossest relations between social setting, access and media portrayal, it does indicate that changes have taken place. These changes in mode of portrayal from no mention, to sensationalism, to less prestigious portrayal are a result of changes in professional values and practices within media as well as changes in public outlooks. Both of these were until recently assumed to be relatively impervious to redefinition.

Some of these changes in media operation and their effect on content have been documented in a variety of studies prepared by NOW media groups. Among these are the fact that many newspapers have introduced new style rules pertaining to women news makers. These have begun to eradicate the worst abuses, such as use of first names, lack of titles and selection of sexually stereotyped details about a woman's looks and clothes. Other ways of changing the perspectives from which stories are covered is to hire more women into the media professions. Guenin documents the fact that women's-page editors have covered the women's movement more often and in greater depth than their male colleagues.[39]

A larger proportion of females in the profession will also help redefine the sex-typed news values operative in the selection of women's issues. Here, Donna Allen, the editor of *Media Report to Women,* has introduced three novel criteria of presentation. They include: no attacks on people, more factual information and let people speak for themselves. "Revolutionary in their simplicity, such ideas would," Dr. Allen notes, "redefine news to include rather than exclude women's activities and redefine the role of the newsperson to be that of a facilitator rather than an interpreter."[40]

The shift in socialization mechanisms noted in the typology, furthermore indicates that a rearrangement of public conceptions about feminism has occurred. The movement from black-out to cooptation and now trivialization suggests that the strong initial resistance has been broken down and that aspects of feminism have become incorporated into the norms and values espoused in the public-discussion agenda. How has this process of rearrangement and legitimation worked?

Burke has drawn attention to the fact that symbolic acts invite consideration rather than overt action. They are thus persuasive devices with the power to rearrange the observer's view of objects.[41] Access or mention on the public-discussion agenda aids in the process of rearrangement in two ways: it legitimates activities and behavior by comparing them with that of other groups and it conveys prestige by providing visibility. The effect of these processes on the presentation of women's issues is exceedingly difficult to pinpoint, but there is some partial documentation in our historical material.

Berger and Luckmann distinguish four levels in the legitimation process to which the media contribute.[42] They are involved on the rhetorical level by transmitting certain ways of talking about human experience, using the vocabulary of equality or inequality, for instance, in portraying sex, status and other differences between groups. In relation to women's issues, it appears that from the 1970 period onward the media publicized women's rights as a legitimate public concern. Though much of the coverage ridiculed women's liberation demands for abolition of marriage, it was nevertheless unable to obfuscate issues like educational and employment equality, which were within the American value structure.[43] The media furthermore supported a climate of expectation that something would be done to alleviate these injustices.

Three additional levels of legitimation are participated in by the media, but these are even more difficult to document. They are the distribution of prevalent legends and maxims, the publication of explicit theories about institutional sectors and the structuring of an all-encompassing historical frame of reference, which links humans to the universe. The patriarchal stereotypes about women's supportive role and beauty and homemaker values to her husband have already been noted as maxims that affect news values. How institutional justifications or general frames of reference affect the reporting of women's issues is, however, not known.

Access or mention in the public-discussion agenda helps the rearrangement of points of view in a second way. It tends to confer status and prestige on those groups associated with public norms. The "grand press blitz" in 1970 made women's liberation the latest media fad and thus legitimated what would otherwise have been seen as an outlandish idea. Moreover, the acceptability of the "older" branch of feminism, including the NOW groups, was increased by having its program and aims compared with the "radical flank" of lesbian, the new left and other groups.[44] Greater public acceptance of such previously taboo subjects as abortion is also reflected in the changing aims of NOW itself, which has become radicalized over time. In 1967 one group split off over repeal of abortion laws, yet four years later abortion law repeal has become a generally accepted plank in the national organization.[45]

Alternate information sources and feminist media-advisory groups have additionally functioned as change agents contributing to the broadening and re-evaluation of the definition of "women's issues." Among these are the newsletters of feminist groups, which constitute part of the underground press, and media outlets owned by feminists. The publication of a slick magazine like MS in 1972, featuring contents about professional, legal, managerial, artistic and single-life options for women has introduced these topics to virtually every other traditional women's magazine on the North American continent. The Feminist Radio Network Inc. has established an alternate news gathering network, which will broaden the agenda of women's issues.[46] The redesigned women's pages, now finally called "Lifestyles" or "Today," have introduced some new topics into the daily press. All these processes together are changing the one-dimensional frames of reference superimposed on women's and men's lives since the advent of the industrial revolution.

NOTES

[1] Edie N. Goldenberg, *Making the Papers* (Lexington: D.C. Heath Co., 1975).

[2] Walter Gieber and Walter Johnson, "The 'City Hall' Beat: A Study of Reporter and Source Roles," *Journalism Quarterly*, 38:2 (Summer 1961), pp. 289–97).

[3] Cynthia Fuchs Epstein, *Woman's Place, Options and Limits in Professional Careers* (Berkeley: University of California Press, 1970).

[4] William Winslow Bowman *Distaff Journalists: Women as a Minority Group in the News Media* (Unpublished Ph.D. Thesis, Chicago Circle: University of Illinois, 1974).

[5] Gertrude Joch Robinson, "Women Journalists in Canadian Dailies: A Social and Professional Minority Profile" (McGill University, 1975).

[6] Linda Busby, "Sex-Role Research in the Mass Media," *Journal of Communication*, 25:4 (Autumn 1975), pp. 107–31.

[7] Gertrude Joch Robinson, "Foreign News Selection is Non-Linear in Yugoslavia's Tanjug Agency," *Journalism Quarterly*, 47:3 (Summer 1970), pp. 340–51.

[8] Warren Breed, "Social Control in the Newsroom: A Functional Analysis," *Social Forces*, 33 (1955), pp. 326–36.

[9] Bernard Roshco, *Newsmaking* (Chicago: University of Chicago Press, 1975), p. 106.

[10] Walter Lippmann, *Public Opinion* (New York: The Free Press, 1922, reprinted in 1965, pp. 54–55.

[11] Roshco, *op. cit.*, p. 112.

[12] Gena Corea, "Writer says papers biased in covering news of women," *Editor and Publisher*, 106 (April 21, 1973), p. 62.

[13] "Sexism in the Country's Largest Newspaper, the New York Daily News," *Media Report to Women*, 2:1 (January 1974), p. 11.

[14] Ben H. Bagdikian, *The Information Machines* (New York: Harper & Row, 1971), Chapter 4.

[15] Zena Beth Guenin, "Women's Pages in American Newspapers," *Journalism Quarterly*, 52:1 (Spring 1975), pp. 66–69, 75.

[16] Corea, *op cit.*, p. 62.

[17] See footnote p. 95.

[18] *Ibid.*, p. 69.

[19] Paul H. Lazarsfeld and Robert K. Merton, "Mass Communication, Popular Taste and Organized Social Action," in Wilbur Schramm, ed., *Mass Communications* (Urbana: University of Illinois Press, 1960, pp. 492–512.

[20] Jo Freeman, *The Politics of Women's Liberation* (New York: David McKay Inc., 1975).

[21] *Ibid.*, pp. 74–75.

[22] Shulamith Firestone, "On American Feminism," in Vivian Gornick and Barbara K. Moran, *Woman in Sexist Society* (New York: Mentor, 1972), pp. 679–86.

[23] Freeman, *op. cit.*, p. 112.

[24] Monica Morris, "Newspapers and the New Feminists: Blackout as Social Control," *Journalism Quarterly,* 50:1 (Winter 1973), pp. 37–42.

[25] Freeman, *op. cit.*, p. 148.

[26] *Ibid.*, p. 114.

[27] Sandre North, "Reporting the Movement," *Atlantic Monthly* (March 1970), pp. 105–6.

[28] Freeman, *op. cit.*, p. 114.

[29] *Ibid.*, pp. 87, 91.

[30] *Ibid.*, pp. 97.

[31] Casey Miller and Kate Swift, *Words and Women, New Language in New Times* (Garden City: Anchor Press/Doubleday, 1976), pp. 13–15.

[32] As reported in Muriel Akamatsu, "Liberating the Media: News," *Freedom of Information Center Report 289* (University of Missouri, September 1972), p. 2.

[33] *Media Report to Women,* 2:1 (January 1974), p. 11, and Akamatsu, *op. cit.*, p. 2.

[34] George Orwell, "The Principles of Newspeak," in *Nineteen Eighty-Four* (New York: Harcourt Brace and Co., 1949), p. 310.

[35] Freeman, *op. cit.*, pp. 71–72.

[36] Joseph Gusfield, *Symbolic Crusade, Status Politics and the American Temperance Movement* (Urbana: University of Illinois Press, 1966), pp. 1–15.

[37] Jo Freeman, "The Origins of the Women's Liberation Movement," in Joan Huber, ed., *Changing Women in a Changing Society* (Chicago: University of Chicago Press, 1973), pp. 38, 42.

[38] Gusfield, *op. cit.*, p. 131.

[39] Zena Beth Guenin, "Women's Pages in the 1970s" *Montana Journalism Review,* 16 (1973), p. 30.

[40] As quoted in "Women's Institute for Freedom of the Press," *Women's Agenda: Women and the Media,* 2:2 (February 1977), p. 11.

[41] G. Burke, *The Grammar of Motives* (New York: Prentice Hall, 1945), p. 393.

[42] Peter Berger and Thomas Luckmann, *The Social Construction of Reality: A Treatise in the Sociology of Knowledge* (Garden City: Doubleday Co., 1967), p. 103.

[43] Freeman, *Politico,* p. 234.

[44] *Ibid.*, p. 234.

[45] *Ibid.*, pp. 80, 98*ff*.

[46] *Media Report to Women,* 2:11 (November 1974), p. 1.

VII

Defining News Organizationally: News Definitions in Practice

by **LEON V. SIGAL**

Wesleyan University

FOR REPORTERS who want to write about women and to do so in ways that reflect the ideologies of the women's movement, women's place is on the women's page in today's daily newspaper. Before dismissing this assertion as the ruminations of an unreconstructed male chauvinist pig, it may be worth examining its basis in the ways that the journalistic community defines news.

If what we mean by a news definition is a relatively succinct statement of criteria to characterize news and to distinguish news from non-news, then there is no such thing. No reporter, no editor or publisher, no critic, in short, nobody knows what news is. Even more troubling, nobody knows what news means. The absence of shared criteria for news—in the journalistic community as well as outside it—is the basis of the fundamental uncertainty that lies at the heart of news making.

Yet, even if we cannot stipulate what news is, we can still define it

109

operationally: news is whatever the news media publish or broadcast. While that seems obvious enough, its implications may be worth considering. If news is defined *in situ,* that is, in the process of making it, then to understand what news is, we must find out how it is made.

The first thing to appreciate about news making is that it is not an individual endeavor but a social one. The streak of frontier individualism evoked in images of a crusading Zenger or a dogged Woodward and Bernstein tends to obscure the point that people who work at news making are, by and large, organization men whose output is processed through complex bureaucratic enterprises and gathered from similar institutions.[1]

Large news organizations like the *Washington Post* and the *New York Times* share all the principal attributes of bureaucracies enumerated by Max Weber. They have a division of labor structured along functional and geographic lines. Functionally, newsmen specialize as news editors, copy editors, general assignment reporters, or reporters covering a specific substantive area such as economics, defense, sports, drama or society. Geographically, they are arranged by desks—foreign, national and metropolitan; in bureaus around the nation and the world; and on beats in various parts of places like Washington or their hometown. They have a hierarchy of authority, at least in a formal sense. They operate with a system of rules, or standard operating procedures, for gathering and transcribing information. Lastly, they have a measure of impersonality: people interact with each other not simply according to who they are as people, but according to what they are inside the organization—according to the jobs they hold.

The first definer of news, then, is the routine of organizational process. Deadlines, leg work and contacts, beats, press releases, press conferences—these are the routines of newsgathering. People in news organizations, says James Reston, "are usually delivering the news as the post office delivers the mail."[2] If so, then we must pay attention to the senders of the messages that news organizations transmit, to the sources of news.

In choosing their news sources, reporters do not act like free-floating atoms in a mass of humanity. They have a social location that limits what they can see and hear and thereby further defines what becomes news. What is news depends upon whether the journalist is a foreign editor or a metropolitan editor; a reporter assigned to cover the Pentagon, the White House or Washington headquarters; a foreign correspondent in London, Cairo or Jerusalem. A critical point in social location is position within the news organization. Position shapes perspective. "Where you stand," Rufus Miles once put it, "depends on where you sit."[3] So does, he might have added, what you see. Position also determines the vantage points journalists have for getting others to see it their way.

In addition to organizational routines and social location, the other definers of news are journalists' habits of mind. Catch phrases, role conceptions and, above all, news-making conventions comprise what may be called "the journalists' creed," transmitted from one generation to the next. "Straight news," or setting down information with a minimum of explicit interpretation; "balance" or "fairness," thereby making news columns accessible to various sides in a political controversy; "authoritative sources," people who are judged reputable enough to quote or to accept information from; "news pegs," timing publication of stories to coincide with discrete events, however staged; and "exclusives," information available to only one reporter or news organization at the time of its publication—these conventions implicitly all provide criteria for selecting information to include in the news.

Social location accounts for much of the variation in the news. To a reporter in the White House press room, what Richard Nixon was doing did not seem the way it did to reporters scanning a police blotter or talking to veteran FBI agents. Their news sources differed; so did their news. Routines and conventions, by contrast, limit variety in the news. Reporters attending the same news conference or picking up the same handout will tend to write more or less the same story. Insofar as reporters on a beat all follow the same routines, the news each uncovers will tend to replicate what the others find. Replicability tends to validate the news they do find. Similarly, adherence to the canons of "objective reporting" may not make the news any more or less truthful, but it is a way of coping with uncertainty: so long as reporters share the same conventions, they will tend to report the same news. Routines and conventions thereby impart a modicum of certitude amid pervasive uncertainty—some small reassurance to ease the insecurity of not knowing what news is or what it means.

Social location, organizational routines and journalistic conventions exert a cumulative impact on news content.

For historical reasons that need not concern us here, the news media have concentrated in New York, Washington and Los Angeles. The largest news organizations have regional bureaus scattered in large cities around the country—the television networks in the five cities where they have owned-and-operated stations, the *Times* and *Post* at roughly a dozen sites. In those cities, reporters cluster around those places where information is routinely disseminated by other institutions, typically government agencies. Those who want to make news would thus do well to locate themselves in New York, Washington or Los Angeles, preferably at or near a reporter's beat. If Jimmy Carter is not about to appoint them to high office, they might arrange to testify at a Congressional hearing or take their case to court. If all else fails, they might pass out leaflets or stage a demonstration in front of the Capitol or the courthouse. There is at least some chance that someone covering police headquarters will report their name and offense when they are booked.

Like other organization men, reporters engaged in newsgathering behave according to established routines, or standard operating procedures. Some routines originated out of a need to coordinate the activities of large numbers of people; others, to restrict the play of individual subjectivity; still others, to economize on staff, time and money. Once in place, routines take on a life of their own: they become "the way things are done" around the organization. In an industry that stresses novelty and change—in a word, what's new—it is important to notice the regular, the habitual, the routine that marks news gathering.

Stories must be set in type, pages composed, several editions printed and delivered. Since each stage of production and distribution depends upon completion of a prior stage, setting and meeting deadlines are essential. For reporters, deadlines impose an arbitrary cutoff to news gathering, an injunction to write up the information that they have in hand and hope to catch up with the rest another day. To the extent that news organizations have identical headlines, they will carry similar news, particularly in the case of late-breaking stories.

The set of routines, or programs, that reporters have for gathering news they call "leg work"—interviewing people either in person or by telephone, rather than poring over documents in a library or analyzing statistical data with a computer. Leg work does not proceed at random. Whatever their assignments, reporters have a group of contacts, potential sources of information cultivated over the years, with whom they talk on a regular basis. A beat is little more than the formal routinizing of periodic checks with a network of contacts.

Every day, editors have a new front page to fill. Every day, reporters have a new deadline to meet. The demand for stories is insatiable. Yet staff, time and money are never in sufficient supply. Under conditions of scarcity, efficiency in news gathering requires that editors assign reporters to beats where information is served up regularly and routinely. On the beat, the routine channels for disseminating news are the press release and the press conference, or briefing. Reporters assinged to a beat, trying to produce stories under pressure of deadlines, are not free to roam or probe at will. Unless editors can spare the manpower to relieve them temporarily from their duties on the beat, spot news will tend to squeeze in-depth investigative reporting or trend stories out of the news.

As a consequence of social location and organizational routines, about one-third of all sources of national and foreign news on page one of the *Washington Post* and the *New York Times* are officials of the United States government passing information through routine channels—press releases, press conferences, and official hearings. So, while the number of women entering the labor force may be declining or accelerating, it will not be news until the Bureau of Labor Statistics issues a press release saying so.

Most journalistic conventions reinforce the impact that social location and organizational routine have on news content. The dictates of "objective reporting," enjoining reporters to write the news "straight," ensures high fidelity transmission of the information passed along to them through routine channels of news gathering. It also permits publication of stories based on the opinions of a single source, so long as that source is in a position to call a press conference or issue a press release on a beat regularly covered by reporters. It virtually guarantees a hearing for those opinions regardless of the reporters' own private judgments of their veracity or validity. The "balance' or "fairness" convention does give those dissenting from the prevailing view in Washington an arguing point in trying to make the news; but at the same time it ensures that backers of administration policy always get a hearing, since they are usually in a better position than their opponents to air accusations of imbalance or unfairness against the news organizations that cover them.

When strictly adhered to, this convention does help to protect the news media against charlatans and hucksters who compete for coverage. Yet it disposes reporters to rely primarily on people in authority for information. Anyone not holding office in an identifiable organization has no claim to publicity. In mass movements as in riots, however, there may be no one in authority. The spokesmen for the movement as well as for the rioters are either self-styled and self-appointed, or they are holders of authority in other institutions, outside interpreters, such as policemen, social scientists and, again, public officials. The decentralization of most ad hoc mass movements, their lack of a unique official spokesman and their need to resort to symbolic acts in order to grab headlines may make them appear less than respectable, programmatically inchoate and unlikely to succeed.

The demand for "exclusives," or "scoops," gives authoritative sources bargaining leverage vis-a-vis reporters. It predisposes reporters to curry favor with those in authority on their beats and editors to run news without checking it with alternative sources before their rivals get hold of it. Perhaps under the competitive conditions of news markets at the turn of the century, scoops did have some effect on circulation and revenues, but any such relationship is today tenuous at best. Yet the exclusive remains the test of reportorial performance, earning some Pulitzer Prizes and promotions in the journalism profession. In the uncertain world of news, what other standard of performance might be more readily measurable than who got the story first?

Why they are in a better position is related to two other journalistic conventions: the "authoritative source" and the "exclusive." In the course of this century, authoritativeness as a news source has become synonymous with authority in large institutions and organizations. As late as the 1920s, personalities such as Charles Lindbergh, Charles Chaplin, Albert Einstein and Babe Ruth qualified as authoritative sources. Their opinions on all sorts of topics were deemed worth quoting, and by implication, worth believing. Yet by 1922, Walter Lippmann could assert in *Public Opinion:*

> The established leaders of any organization have a great natural advantage. They are believed to have better sources of information. The books and papers are in their offices. They took part in the important conferences. They met the important people. They have responsibility. It is, therefore, easier for them to secure attention and to speak in a convincing tone.[4]

As the press increasingly organized its news gathering around governmental institutions, moreover, authoritativeness began to vary with distance from positions of formal authority over public policy. Today, the higher up in government a person is, the better his prospects of making the news. On beats around Washington, the emphasis on authoritative sources means that editors hold reporters responsible for covering senior officials in their agency. On the White House beat, this means "covering the body," following the President's very movement. By virtue of his responsibility for public policy, the President has become *the* authoritative source in American journalism.

To the extent that social location, organizational routines and journalistic conventions define what news is in practice, news tends to be what high officials in the American government say it is. It is only by transcending the confines of routine and conventional news gathering that other people have their say and other issues make the news. It is only in those corners of the newsroom that are relatively less restricted by beats and routine channels that reporters themselves have more to say about what is news. One of those places is currently the women's or society page, often renamed the "Style" section to keep up with the trend. There, the exploded concept of what is news allows women relative freedom to write what they want and to do so in the ideological trappings that they prefer. So long as women are denied positions in American society that would qualify them as authoritative sources of news, women's place will remain on the women's page.

NOTES

[1] For a more extensive treatment of some organizational perspectives on the news, see Leon V. Sigal, *Reporters and Officials: The Organization and Politics of Newsmaking* (Lexington, Mass.: Lexington Books, 1973).

[2] James Reston, *The Artillery of the Press* (New York: Harper and Row, 1967), p. 64.

[3] Quoted in Graham T. Allison, *Essence of Decision* (Boston: Little Brown, 1971), p. 176, and attributed to Miles by Herbert Kaufman.

[4] Walter Lippmann, *Public Opinion* (New York: Free Press, 1965), pp. 157–58.

VIII

News Definitions and Their Effects on Women

by **SUZANNE PINGREE** and
ROBERT P. HAWKINS
University of Wisconsin—Madison

I**T IS OUR PURPOSE** here to consider what definitions of news have to say about women, how existing definitions of news might affect various groups of women, and what changes might lead to more equitable coverage of women and women's issues in the press. As social scientists, we will report evidence on these issues whenever possible; however, since this area has not been the subject of a great deal of research, there will also be numerous opportunities for us to speculate about how things might work, given what we know from research in other areas.

DEFINITIONS OF WOMEN'S NEWS

We begin by considering definitions of news or newsworthiness from the point of view of the news audience. That is, we will leave aside (for the moment) the numerous rigorous and not-so-rigorous attempts that have been made to define what is news, and instead see what the content of the press seems to be saying news is. What is the *de facto* definition of news available in the American press as it relates to women? This may be the real heart of the "what is newsworthy" problem, anyway. Do we really care how editors or reporters or publishers think they define news and newsworthiness if that stated definition differs from what they actually put into the paper or on the air? For those concerned about how news definitions affect women, it is surely more direct to examine implicit definitions in the *actual* content and layout of the press than it is to rely on the stated *intentions* of reporters and editors.

Several content analyses of American newspapers provide us with a picture of women's treatment in the press, and several aspects of these results are most significant.[1] First, do we find stories about women, and if so, where? Based on observation of nine Washington, D.C., and Virginia newspapers (including the *Washington Post*), the National Organization for Women found:[2]

1. Nearly all of the writers of news were males (even 75% of the stories on the front page of the "Style" section were written by males.
2. Hard news about women often appeared on the women's pages rather than appropriate news sections.
3. 83% of the obituaries were of males, and males outnumbered females in numbers, column inches and pictures in the obituaries.

While we wouldn't want to devote a lot of time to this last curious fact, it does cause one to wonder if more men than women are dying out there! Perhaps women never die, they just fade away.

Similarly, Susan Miller's study of the content of news photos in the *Washington Post* and the *Los Angeles Times* found that:[3]

1. Most news photos show only men.
2. This was true for each section of the newspapers, with the exception of the "lifestyle" section, where photographs of women were in a slight majority.
3. Males were primarily shown as professionals, public officials, sports figures, entertainers and socialites/celebrities.
4. Females were primarily shown as wives, socialites/celebrities, professionals, entertainers and as objects of human interest.

In other words, women are scarce in the first sections of these newspapers: they are infrequently the subjects of stories or photographs and even less frequently the writers of stories. They do appear more prominently in the "Lifestyle" sections, but if first section coverage is "hard news," one could argue that events with women as major characters are simply not hard news.

A second possible characteristic of how a newspaper defines women's news is whether and where it covers events and issues of women's rights. Monica Morris' study of two Los Angeles County newspapers over the course of a year (1968–69) found: [4]

> Of more than a quarter million units of news, only 26 were devoted to the women's movement.

Other studies of how the press covers social issues in general have sometimes included women's rights as one of these social issues. G. Ray Funkhouser studied ten-year trends (1960–70) of prominent issues in three weekly news magazines—*Time, Newsweek* and *U.S. News and World Reports*. Over the ten-year period, women's rights received scant coverage—usually around 1% of the articles on prominent issues were devoted to women's rights—until 1970, when nearly 8% of these articles dealt with women's rights. [5]

1960	1961	1962	1963	1964	1965	1966	1967	1968	1969	1970
2%	1%	0%	2%	1%	1%	1%	1%	0%	1%	8%

Similarly, a study by Ryan and Owen analyzed the content of eight daily newspapers randomly selected from those papers with a circulation of 300,000 or more. [6] They found that most coverage of social issues was from staff writers, not the wire services. Averaged across papers, the combined category of racism/sexism averaged around 7% of the total coverage devoted to social issues, which itself took up only about 9% of the newshole. Apparently, social issues in general, and women's rights in particular, receive scant coverage in the American press.

Percent of social issues coverage devoted to racism/sexism (approximate figures, adapted from Ryan and Owen, 1976):

Newspaper	Percent
Chicago Daily News	1%
Chicago Tribune	5%
Cleveland Plain Dealer	5%
Cleveland Press	6%
Detroit News	17%
Milwaukee Journal	7%
Philadelphia Inquirer	5%
Washington Post	3%

A third way of looking at newspapers' implicit definitions of news is to examine the content of the one newspaper section that does focus on women—the traditional "women's" section, now often renamed something like "Lifestyle." Critics of this section have called it a ghetto; others have described it as a "dumping ground for anything the male editors consider a 'woman's' story."[7] Others, Gaye Tuchman,[8] for example, have suggested it as a good resource for social movements like the women's rights movement.

Just what does seem to be newspapers' definition of "women's news"? Two studies have looked at this section of American newspapers for changes in response to criticism. Both researchers were interested to know whether the content of these sections had changed, or just their names. Zena Guenin[9] found traditional content more common in women's sections than in the renamed lifestyle section (traditional content being advice, astrology, beauty, brides, charity benefits, clubs, fashion, food, home furnishings and society events). However, the modernized lifestyle sections differed from the traditional women's sections largely in that they seemed to replace traditional content with entertainment content (stories about movies, books, theater, travel, arts and entertainers). This is not what critics of traditional women's sections had in mind!

Similarly, another study by Susan Miller did not find major changes over a ten-year period in the content of the lifestyle sections in four major American newspapers (the *New York Times, Washington Post, Chicago Tribune,* and *Los Angeles Times*), except that they were reduced in size, with a corresponding increase in the size of the paper's entertainment section.[10] Of the four papers, only the *New York Times* seems to have made a real effort to upgrade the pages into a section that adequately considers the problems of both sexes' lifestyles in the 1970s.

Tuchman, in a case study of the *Times'* "women's page,"[11] reports that its editor insists it should carry "news about women, not news for women." This means some coverage of the women's movement, "the changes in women's lives and the effects of the women's movement." Tuchman points out that the women's section is well-suited to this kind of issue information, since most news on the page is "soft"—it's not gathered by interaction with recognized news generating institutions, and is not quickly dated. In addition, when stories about the women's movement are placed here, they can be longer and better displayed. Thus, finding most news concerning women in this section may be at worst a mixed blessing: unfortunately, there seems to be an editorial distinction between news and women's news reminiscent of the English language distinction between people and women; fortunately, there is a women's section in most papers in which at least some content about women can appear.

To summarize these findings, women are scarce in the first sections of American newspapers; in fact, they are scarce everywhere but in the women's or lifestyle sections of papers. Women's rights as a social issue do not receive much coverage either in absolute terms or in terms of the total newshole devoted to issues, which itself is very small. Finally, much of the information present in newspapers where women figure prominently is in the women's or lifestyle section. Most evidence about the renamed versions of these sections suggests that they remain traditional in their content, emphasizing recipes, advice, and social events and such, and are either shortened or contain more entertainment content.

News Definitions and Women's News

Now the obvious question is: "Where do these patterns come from?" While the simple answer has a certain appeal, we probably can't blame all, or even very much, of these biases against women in the news on simple, conscious malevolence (male chauvinism) by male reporters and editors. The very suggestion brings cries of injured innocence from the accused, and most of them are probably quite sincere. But the biases against women in news coverage and the lack of coverage of women and women's issues *are* there and must come from somewhere.

Not surprisingly, we suspect these biases derive in large part from the application of news definitions of women and women's concerns. Two other chapters in this book examine the sources of news definitions and the implications of these definitions for women in some detail, while our main job is to discuss the *effects* of news definitions. Still, a few words here about our conceptions of news definitions and their implications for women may make clearer what follows.

It seems almost a truism that news is one of those intangibles that is impossible to define. And it is true that no matter what definition is proposed, someone will quickly point out its exceptions and omissions. As we see it, however, these disagreements will probably not be resolved by the finding of the "right" or even an adequate definition of news, because such a definition may not even be possible. "News" is not an entity with an existence of its own so that we can hope to eventually pin it down. Instead, our ability to judge something as "news," or even to place it on a continuum of "newsworthiness," results from the *intersection* of a variety of qualities: professional ideologies, rules or goals (themselves sometimes taken to define news in a narrower sense); social attitudes, economics of news gathering and transmission; organizational psychology and sociology; habit and so on. Thus, "news" or "newsworthiness" is a concept derived from a large and ill-defined set of other concepts. Any attempt to define news will be an argument about two points: what attributes or processes are relevant to the definition of news, and what are the relative weights of contributing concepts or decision rules about which combinations constitute news and which do not. Therefore, instead of waiting for *a* definition to emerge, a more reasonable course seems to be to approach a working consensus over what is more-or-less a definition of news through an examination of the individual factors that influence either what editors say is news or what is actually in papers and newscasts.

A number of the factors that would be prominent on many observers' lists probably have a great deal to do with why coverage (or non-coverage) of women is the way it is. For example, despite frequent cries for more issue-oriented news, we already know that 91% of news copy on eight major papers was event-oriented,[12] and this should not surprise us. As Bernard Roshco points out in his cogent book, *Newsmaking*,[13] the basic function of news is to keep us *aware,* not necessarily knowledgeable, of *what is going on* in the world. But starting with this functional premise then requires us to regard reporting that interprets, explains and fosters understanding as secondary or "soft" news—we only need it in order to interpret the event-oriented news, and it is events that are "going on" after all.

Part of the problem women and women's issues have had (a problem shared with minority groups, consumer movements, ecology groups and such) is that much of what we would like to see reported is never event-news at all. The myriad forms of oppression of women did not suddenly begin by Presidential decree last Thursday; they have been around for hundreds of years and have been adapted gradually as changing social and technological circumstances required. The ways in which couples are managing two jobs, children, housekeeping, *and* self-respect and sanity are not events that demand immediate publication because of their recency (and they don't evolve overnight, either!). Regardless of significance, continuing conditions, plans, strategies or potential solutions to problems are not news events, although announcement, confirmation or announced support of them can be.

A simplistic response to the predicament might be to say that it's our own fault if we're caught in this trap. After all, if one wants newspaper and television coverage, and if the press covers events and not issues, aren't we being pig-headed to pin our hopes on coverage of issues and conditions we think important? Shouldn't we be content to be covered when we participate in and shape the events of the day, like any other news makers? The problem with this argument is that it ignores the imbalance of power among potentially significant groups and individuals. Often the most significant thing about those in power *is* what they have done, because their actions can affect many other people's lives. Those without power ordinarily cannot, be definition, take such actions. What is significant about them is their powerlessness, their oppression and their struggles to remedy these conditions. But even their struggles, unless they choose to go "outside the system," are a series of small, gradual events with little immediate significance for a wider public. Thus, women as potential news makers are placed in a very difficult position by this aspect of a definition of news: most women are denied the decision-making power that would make their actions news, and without power and the consequent prominence, only their most obtrusive actions are newsworthy.

A related problem for women stems from news-gathering organizations' needs for economic efficiency. Placing reporters on beats where news is deemed most likely to occur (e.g., the White House, police headquarters) produces more stories per person-hour invested than scattering them throughout the city. Quite obviously, this practice is at least partly responsible for the constant stream of stories on essentially trivial Presidential activities (e.g., "the President admitted today that he often has a snack of peanuts before going to bed"). Equally so, the beat structure ensures that we will be informed of all major crimes, fires and accidents. But from the point of view of women and women's issues, generally not on a news beat, the beat structure serves as an additional hurdle. To paraphrase a current saying about women's abilities and job success, a woman has to be twice as newsworthy as a man to get the same coverage.

We mentioned before that reporters and editors probably do not consciously discriminate against women and women's issues in the selection of news, and indeed conscious discrimination is not necessary with the beat structure, power imbalances and an issue-orientation all working against women. But there is at least one further unconscious or incidental way that reporters and editors themselves form a barrier to women in the news, and that is through their perceptions of their audiences. Presidents, movie stars, and beautiful people are not a constant presence in the news simply because of the beat structure or their power to affect others with their actions. They are also there because of their relevance to us (for whatever reason) and what editors believe (and can often demonstrate) to be our interest in them. Thus, out of what has *happened* involving *powerful* people in conventional, *predictable* situations and positions, newspapers are sold and ratings built by trying to give the audience news that is relevant to its needs or, equivalently, of interest to it.

Here one might argue that women are probably no worse off than any other significant issue such as news of a famine that is cut out for a story on a movie star's divorce. But an additional bias against women and women's issues may be built in by the simple fact that reporters and editors are almost all males. And while there is relatively little evidence on this point, it is very easy to imagine how these men could unintentionally exclude women from the news by being most willing to consider newsworthy those topics they themselves are interested in and affected by, or that loom large in their own attitude structures. Furthermore, audience interest is usually not directly assessed, but only presumed to be known, and news selections are made on the basis of those presumptions. Research on the psychology of sex roles has amply shown that caricature-like stereotypes of the sexes are widely accepted, especially by men,[14] so these presumptions of interest are probably based on stereotypes of women much more than on any appreciation of what today's women think is important or find interesting (to argue that ratings or circulation guard against such misperceptions misses the point that there are no ratings of untried content). Thus, women in non-traditional occupations, legal rights, crisis centers and such, all run the risk of exclusion because "our typical woman reader is a housewife who isn't interested in that lib stuff."

One study of communication students simulated this situation by asking the students to rate the interest of women, men and the general public in a variety of potential news categories.[15] Not surprisingly, men were seen as more interested than women in politics, science, business and sports, while women were believed to be more interested in cooking, fashion and religion. Female students made less use of sex role stereotypes in making the ratings, suggesting that women reporters and editors would be less likely to make sex-typed assumptions about the interests of their readers, and thus would be more ready to present non-traditional content.

Our final characteristic of the news definition process that is especially relevant to women is somewhat of a paradox coming after these findings, since women reporters and editors (or at least women-oriented ones) in at least one situation contribute to the dearth of hard news about women. Leon Sigal's study of the front-page makeup at the *New York Times* and the *Washington Post*,[16] and informant evidence cited by Gaye Tuchman,[17] clearly demonstrate how much news decisions are based on internal political struggles between editors competing to get their reporters' stories into the paper (or an apportioning of space to avoid a struggle). Typically, the "geographically based" editors—national, foreign, metropolitan—are much more powerful than "topically based" editors—women's sports, culture—by virtue of the amount of hard news in their fiefs. Thus, "topically based" editors have a hard time getting their stories on the front page even if they manage to overcome the other problems posed by the "softness" of much of the news in their area.

The paradox comes from Tuchman's report that on the *New York Times,* the women's-page editor and her staff deliberately avoid competing for scarce front-page space so that stories they consider important can be given expansive, picture-laden, issue-oriented coverage on the women's page. Their argument, to which we will return later, is that full coverage with reader-catching photos buried deep in the paper is preferable to the snippet on the front page that provides little real information. But it is clear that their conscious decisions, motivated at least in part by feminism, may contribute to the lack of coverage of women and women's issues elsewhere in the paper.

The question at this point is properly "so what?" So coverage of women and women's issues in the news is scanty and has identifiable biases. So it probably stems at least in part from certain characteristics of the way in which news is defined. What we really need to know is what difference these biases make, and why.

EFFECTS ON THE AUDIENCE

Our approach to this question of what differences these biases make is based on the importance of the mass media in the construction of social reality. As Gaye Tuchman argues:

> In their attitudes, in their social organization, in their identifications of events as news, the news media are part and parcel of the society they serve. Although they claim to be merely a mirror to the world, that "mirror" might be better described as part of a reciprocal relationship between the news media and their environment. The news media are both "a cause" and "an effect."[18]

What we mean by this is that the mass media in general, and the news media particularly, are constantly presenting us with symbolic messages about what "reality" is like, and we use these messages in constructing our own images of reality. Even news media institutions are not immune. It is in this sense a reciprocal relationship: what is important is news, and what is in the news is important. We would go even further than Tuchman here, and argue that these symbolic messages do not reflect the real world accurately; if the media act as a mirror, the mirror is a distorted one.[19] We shall use the general findings of the content analyses reported earlier to illustrate these points.

Discovering that news stories about women are largely absent from the first sections of newspapers is not in itself what we mean by "symbolic message." This fact, fairly easily verifiable, does not uniquely imply any one meaning. However, the symbolic message is the meaning that most people would apply to the fact that women are largely absent from hard-news sections of newspapers. In developing an analysis of the fictional world of television prime time, George Gerbner and Larry Gross argue that the symbolic message of presence or absence works this way:

> Representation in the fictional world signifies social existence; absence means symbolic annihilation.[20]

If you are present, you are important; if you are absent, you are insignificant. This is very like Lazarsfeld and Merton's "status conferral" function of the media.[21] This probable meaning, or symbolic message, implies an effect, and Gerbner and Gross find evidence for this kind of effect in a variety of ways in their cultivation analyses.[22] When heavy television viewers are compared to light television viewers in their responses to questions about reality, heavy viewers of television tend to show a "television bias." For example, content analyses show that Americans are over-represented on prime time television and that foreigners are under-represented. When asked a question about what proportion of the world's population Americans represent, heavy viewers are likelier to give a response reflecting the biased content of television: they overestimate. Other cultivation analyses have dealt with the prevalence of violence, prevalence of occupations, and altruism/self-interest as motives for behavior.

Returning to the scarcity of women in the news, if we asked the audience to estimate the proportion of women in the population, an underestimate or one very far from 50–50 would be unlikely, because it is a highly visible fact and one of everyday knowledge that women are 51% of the population in the United States. With the basic fact in mind that there are *not* more men than women in the world, an audience confronted with the disproportion in news media attention to men might conclude that men are more important, more worthy of attention than women; or they might conclude that men are more involved in the significant events of the world; or simply that men's activities are news and women's are not.

Similarly, the failure of the press to give attention to the women's rights movement as a social issue carries with it a symbolic message about the importance of the movement. However, basic facts about general support for civil rights for women are more ambiguous than are basic facts about numbers of women and men—it's harder to tell whether people agree with the sometimes complex arguments and issues of the movement than it is to understand a basic fact about the population. Because of this, the symbolic message is likely to be two-fold: the movement is not an important one worthy of a great deal of news media attention *and* there is not a great deal of support out there for the movement.

We come to a somewhat different situation in considering what the meaning of the "women's" or lifestyle section of the paper might be. It is clear that women are a majority here, although not to the extent that men are in the other sections. It is also clear that, with some notable exceptions, much of the content of these sections is aimed at the interests of the traditional woman. The fact that there is a "womens" section may be the most powerful message of all that the news is for and about men: how odd to think of one separate section for half the population, while the rest of the paper is for the other half. To make this point plainer, imagine labeling the parts of the paper directed stereotypically at men (sports, business, politics)[23] as "men's" sections. The message seems to have several parts: first, this section of the paper is for women; second, it is *not* for men; third, women are "separate but equal"—it's all right for them to appear in the newspaper, but only within their traditional section of the paper.

One implication of this message is that men will probably not read the "women's " section, especially when it is labeled this way. Sandra and Daryl Bem have demonstrated in their research with sex-segregated want ads that something as simple as a label can make a difference like this.[24] They found both sexes to be more interested in traditionally cross-sex jobs when they were not labeled as such: that is, women were more interested in a job that was unlabeled than when it was listed under "Help Wanted—Male."

Another implication of labeling one section "women's" is that we are encouraged to think of women as a special class of people, indeed, as distinct from people (and, given the size of this section compared to the rest of the paper, less important people). When this is coupled with traditional content in the "women's" section, the message is obvious that a woman's place is different from a man's, less significant, and it is in the home. There is now fairly substantial evidence that such content in other media does affect the audience,[25] and there is no reason to expect that it doesn't here as well. One could even argue that what is in the paper has *more* effect than what we read in novels or see on television: the newspaper is supposed to be real, these other media are not. If we are using the media to construct social reality, we should be relying more heavily on reality-oriented content.[26]

If, on the other hand, the "women's" section of the paper is used to present information about the status of women and the progress of efforts to improve their status, some of these negative effects may be balanced. It is true that putting news about this civil rights issue in one section may carry with it the unfortunate idea that the women's movement is only for and about women, and that women's rights are not important issues. However, this does insure that it will appear in the paper, and that's better than no coverage. It can also become a power base for future integration. If the ultimate goal is integration of stories about women into the rest of the paper, then at least one strategy is to develop a central source of these stories and attempt to get them placed elsewhere in the paper. Also, to the extent that these stories appear in the "women's" section, they will replace traditional content, or at least provide an alternative to it. At the very least, the "separate but equal" woman will see a wider range of options open to her, and the interested man will find some content relevant to his needs in a changing society.

To summarize, the lack of coverage of women and the placement of what coverage there is has a clear potential to affect the news audience. Beyond the obvious effect that the audience will remain uninformed about women and women's issues, the implicit symbolic messages contained in the coverage largely serve to reinforce cultural stereotypes about the insignificance of women and their "proper place."

At this point, we would like to emphasize that this effect is not omnipotent. It doesn't necessarily work this way for all members of the audience. In fact, the coverage of the women's movement is a good example of an exception: despite what we have shown as a nearly complete absence of information about women's rights in the press in the 1960s, the National Organization for Women was formed in the mid-sixties, and the movement got very much underway.

EFFECTS ON JOURNALISTS

One effect of news definitions on journalists is of course obvious—the definitions determine what events the reporter will be sent to cover, define what sorts of information should be obtained and guide the format of presentation. However, a less obvious but no less important effect is on the reporter's own construction of social reality. For one thing, reporters are part of the audience for news, and should be susceptible to the same sorts of effects on their perceptions of the social significance of women and women's issues. In fact, reporters may even be more susceptible than the general public. Since the ability to distinguish significant people and events from the non-significant is an asset in their work, the significance of women is useful in their work instead of being just incidental information.

News definitions themselves work to the same effect, and more directly. The rules and practices of news gathering are not simply an arbitrary system of conventions for a craft to follow, but explicitly purport to locate what is timely and significant. Since we have seen that these conventions systematically exclude women from news pages and broadcasts, it would be surprising if reporters and editors did not quickly form general social attitudes about the insignificance of women that serve as a further bar to women's news and probably to women reporters as well.[27]

News definitions also make it difficult for a feminist reporter (female or male) to personally do anything about the biases against women's news; since the conventions define what is significant, the reporter is restrained seemingly for a good reason from covering what she/he might like to do. To be willing to break the conventions and cover women and women's issues anyway requires some insight into the fact that the conventions act as much to define and confer significance as to simply locate existing significance. Beyond that, such a reporter must *already* have established a reputation for sound news judgment in conventional terms in order for his/her departure to be accepted. Basically, then, the effects of news definitions on reporters derive from the fact that they must learn and operate within a system of conventions that tend to limit coverage of women, and that the conventions provide symbolic messages about women that can easily be incorporated into reporters' own social attitudes.

STRATEGIES FOR CHANGE

We have already implicitly described the effects of news definitions on women news makers; for a variety of reasons, they are systematically excluded from the newspapers and from broadcast news reports. Important but obvious corollary effects probably include doubt in the worthwhileness of what one is doing and/or frustration at one's inability to get news coverage. But potential news makers who are women are also the affected group who probably most want to change things, and we will suggest some ways in which women could get more news coverage.

Before turning to strategies for getting women and women's issues covered as news, we would like to pose a question to be borne in mind. We can demonstrate a lack of coverage and we can suggest some likely effects of this lack, but we need to ask ourselves: "Why do we want to be in the news?" Is it to present our oppression and struggle to a wide audience to gain support and build up our political clout? Or is it that we want confirmation from the prestige-granting media that we are significant? If our reasons are primarily the latter, then it is the *fact* of coverage and where that coverage occurs that concerns us most. But if we want coverage in order to gain support, then we must be concerned with the depth and fullness of stories—*what* is to be covered.

The first and most obvious and least useful way to achieve both goals is by having more women news makers, given conventional definitions of news. If half the Wall Street brokers, half the legislators, half the business executives, and half the Supreme Court and so on were women, then women would begin to be in the news. Women would be on the beat system, making decisions in positions of power so that their actions would meet conventional criteria for news coverage as timely events relevant to the broad public. Or to put it another way, if women weren't discriminated against in society as a whole, we would no longer need to worry about the effects of news definitions on women. Of course, that's not a very satisfying solution, since it so thoroughly puts the cart of our entire society before what we think may be the horse of the news media. Since we wouldn't be focusing on the news media in the first place if we didn't consider them pivotal in social change, we need to find ways to change media coverage *in order to* hasten the changes we want in society.

However, the notion of changing coverage of women by a work force change does make some sense if we limit ourselves to getting more women as reporters and editors. Women journalists probably are less stereotyped in the interests they ascribe to their audience, and also more likely to share interests with the women in their audience, and both these characteristics probably will lead to more coverage of women. Grace Lichtenstein, former head of the *New York Times* Rocky Mountain bureau, reports that she initiated a page-one story on changes in rape laws around the country; the changes met conventional news criteria, but male editors hadn't thought of it, and had been closely following capital punishment.[28] Naturally, sheer numbers of women reporters can only solve part of this problem if their stories are always judged for audience interest by editors with stereotyped notions, so we need people who do not share these stereotypes in high-ranking journalism positions as well. However, while this solution is more finite than changing all of society, it too still has two drawbacks. First, it is a relatively long-term solution of little comfort to the feminist with an issue to publicize now. And second, there is relatively little that feminist news makers can hope to do to get non-sexist journalists hired and promoted (although the rare woman news maker whose views are newsworthy because she herself is newsworthy or because her actions will put her in legal jeopardy can demand a non-sexist interviewer).

There are two more direct and immediate options available to the potential news maker who feels ignored by the media, one much used with varying degrees of success, and the other practically unutilized. First, if one is having a hard time getting one's issue-news covered, the widely used tactic is to tie that issue to an event. A march, a noon rally with speakers outside the State legislature, pickets in front of a supermarket, the famous bra-burning that evidently never happened—all of these are more-or-less obtrusive events whose organizers generally do not believe have any direct significance.[29] Its purpose is usually explicitly to call attention to or to symbolize the issue that is the real matter of concern. The hope is that the event will force coverage and that the coverage will present the issue that was the purpose behind the event. Often socially-aware reporters will carefully try to get some statement that sums up the issue behind the event, and then the organizers will probably be at least partially satisfied, although they will probably wish the issue had gotten more air time or column inches and the pseudo-event less.

This tactic contains limitations and pitfalls, however, and its use calls for creativity, realistic expectations and balance. Even though the organizers may be intending to get coverage for an issue, it is their pseudo-event that makes them newsworthy, so there is no guarantee that the issue itself will get more than a mention. Also, the more obtrusive, unusual or outrageous the pseudo-event, the more likely it is to be covered, but also the more likely it is to be ridiculed in the news presentation or seen as over-reacting. Finally, the news maker should know what she expects to achieve. If the goal is to convey information about the issue—why it's important, what the arguments are—then the pseudo-event may have little value, since such statements are likely to get lost in the trivial happenings of the event. However, if her goals have more to do with demonstrating social significance of the issue and its supporting movement, and if she is willing to rely on other channels of communication to provide more substantive information, the pseudo-event may be ideal. For example, when 20,000 supporters of the ERA march on the State Capitol, it is unlikely that their reasons or arguments will get front-page coverage, although they may be described in a feature inside the paper or in a news special. But the fact that 20,000 people marched will be reported on the front page with the clear message that the issue is an important one with substantial support. So, the use of pseudo-events to obtain coverage of one's issues can be effective, if one's goals are the simple signification of importance. However, we reiterate that its use is definitely to be approached as an art form, not a science.

The other strategy available to potential women news makers is to change the journalists' stereotyped perceptions of what the audience wants. One very expensive way to do this is to set up a competing media outlet that provides all the content your nemesis does, plus the issue content you want. As you make some dent in their ratings or circulation, they will probably fight back by copying you to take away your small competitive advantage. Whereupon you will be forced out of business but will have achieved your goal. This sort of Pyrrhic victory could only be indulged in by those with vast personal fortunes, but fortunately there are less expensive ways to make the point.

We suggest telling them what you're interested in and what you aren't; what you find offensive and how they could avoid it. Most editors are aware that they don't get much feedback from their communities and that what they do get is probably not representative. Of course, our potential women news maker or organization (preferably the organization) isn't representative either, but those who do speak out carry disproportionate weight. And mass media outlets do like to think of themselves as serving their communities, and are even willing to sacrifice small amounts of profitable time and space to make themselves feel good. This is probably especially true of broadcast media, since they have a watchdog (admittedly fairly toothless, but stations often act as if they don't know it) in the FCC seeing to it that they "serve the public interest."

What it comes down to is that the reporters and editors often simply do not know that there are women interested in more than recipes and dirty collars, and if they do know that there are some "libbers" around, they probably don't know what the "libbers" really want—after all, all they know is what they read in the papers. One way to let them know is to simply talk with them, quietly and reasonably.

We have to admit that this notion more or less fell into our laps.

The General Manager of one of the Madison, Wisconsin, television stations attended a NOW-sponsored discussion of media stereotypes and said he was willing to talk further about it. Surprised, the NOW chapter formed a Media Task Force with us as co-chairs and we began meeting with the General Manager and various members of his staff. It took some months of sporadic meetings, but gradually they saw that we weren't there simply to attack them (although we did when we thought they deserved it) but to try to find reasonable and inexpensive ways for them to provide better coverage of women and avoid inadvertent sexism. For our part, we came to realize that the things we objected to in their coverage did not stem from intentional sexism, but from some unexamined assumptions about women.

Two of us went to one of the monthly breakfast meetings of the news staff to answer their questions about how we thought they should handle sensitive stories and about which terms we found offensive. We suggested a number of possible women's shows they could produce locally, and they did adopt one and showed it at noon one Tuesday when the network gave them back a half-hour. Finally, in spring 1976 they adopted as station policy a six-page memorandum we prepared outlining guidelines for non-sexist programming and advertising practices (available from Madison NOW), and have sent a one-page summary of these guidelines to all their advertisers. Emboldened by our success, we approached the other two commercial stations in Madison and found that they too were willing to sit down and discuss things—both have since adopted the same guidelines, although our relationships with them have not yet reached the relaxed stage they have with the first station.

Has it made any difference? We think it has. We no longer hear snide anti-feminist comments as small talk between stories—sometimes we even hear the sort of snide comments *we* would make about a story! Recently, coverage of a series of rape-attacks was full, sensitive and responsible (we had just met with "our" station the week before). These may sound like small changes, but we think they are very important ones. And this sort of consciousness-raising activity can be carried out by the relatively small core of active movement members—it doesn't need to turn out masses of people.

In closing, we probably should add that there is one more place to look for changes that might affect women's issues, and that is in the explicit conventions and ideologies of news. In recent years there has been a running debate in journalism between neutral and participant ideologies, with the neutral ideology corresponding to classical objectivity, and the participant ideology arguing for interpretive reporting, background stories, and even advocacy for those without power in society.[30] Obviously, the women's movement has much to gain if the participant position gains further respectability, although the advocacy aspect may now be in some disrepute. But we think that at least part of the participant philosophy is gaining respectability and may be a point one can tap in discussions with reporters and editors.

Still, the position of women and women's issues with respect to the news is not terribly good, even at best. Even if a participant approach to journalism becomes more respectable and flourishes, such writing is likely in the forseeable future to remain subordinate to "hard" news—a recounting of the day's events. And even with hard-working and clever women trying to put their issues before the public through pseudo-events and through discussions with news editors, one basic fact still leaves women and women's issues at a disadvantage: Until women are no longer discriminated against in society as a whole, they will continue to face an uphill battle to put themselves and their issues before the general public.

NOTES

[1] Most of these results are summarized in greater detail in Matilda Butler and William Paisley, *Women and the Mass Media,* forthcoming.

[2] National Organization for Women, Northern Virginia Chapter. A survey of the *Washington Post* newspaper. March, 1973.

[3] Susan H. Miller. "The Content of News Photos: Women's and Men's Roles," *Journalism Quarterly,* 52 (1975), pp. 68–73.

[4] This result was taken from a re-analysis by Butler and Paisley, *op. cit.,* of Monica Morris, "Newspapers and the New Feminists: Black Out as Social Control?" *Journalism Quarterly,* 50 (1973), pp. 37–42.

[5] G. Ray Funkhouser, "Trends in Media Coverage of the Issues of the '60s," *Journalism Quarterly,* 50 (1973), pp. 533–38.

[6] Michael Ryan and Dorothea Owen, "A Content Analysis of Metropolitan Newspaper Coverage of Social Issues," *Journalism Quarterly,* 54 (1976), pp. 634–40.

[7] Lindsy Van Gelder, "Women's Pages: You Can't Make News Out of a Silk Purse," *Ms.,* 3 (1974), pp. 112–16.

[8] Gaye Tuchman, "The Newspaper as a Social Movement's Resource," in Gaye Tuchman, Arlene K. Daniels and James Benet, eds., *Home and Hearth: Images of Women in the Media* (New York: Oxford University Press, 1977).

[9] Zena Beth Guenin, "Women's Pages in American Newspapers: Missing Out on Contemporary Content," *Journalism Quarterly,* 52 (1975), pp. 66–69.

[10] Susan H. Miller, "Changes in Women's/Lifestyle Sections," *Journalism Quarterly,* 54 (1976), p. 641.

[11] Gaye Tuchman, *op. cit.*

[12] Michael Ryan and Dorothea Owen, *op. cit.*

[13] Bernard Roshco, *Newsmaking* (Chicago: University of Chicago Press, 1975).

[14] See, for example, V. Flerx, D. Fidler and R. Rogers, "Sex Role Stereotypes: Developmental Aspects and Early Intervention, *Child Development,* 47 (1976), pp. 998–1007; E. Maccoby and C. Jacklin, *The Psychology of Sex Differences* (Stanford: Stanford University Press, 1974); S. Pingree, "The Effects of Nonsexist Television Commercials and Perceptions of Reality on Children's Attitudes about Women," *Psychology of Women Quarterly,* in press.

[15] Jack Orwant and Muriel Cantor, "How Sex Stereotyping Affects Perceptions of News Preferences," *Journalism Quarterly,* 54 (1977), pp. 99–108.

[16] Leon Sigal, *Reporters and Officials.* (Lexington, Mass.: Lexington Books, 1973).

[17] Gaye Tuchman, *op. cit.*

[18] Gaye Tuchman, *op. cit.*

[19] Matilda Butler and William Paisley, *op. cit.*

[20] George Gerbner and Larry Gross, "Living with Television: The Violence Profile," *Journal of Communication* (Spring 1976), p. 182.

[21] Paul Lazarsfeld and Robert Merton, "Mass Communication, Popular Taste, and Organized Social Action," in Wilbur Schramm and Donald F. Roberts,

The Process and Effects of Mass Communication (Urbana: University of Illinois Press, 1971).

[22] George Gerbner and Larry Gross, *op. cit.*

[23] Jack Orwant and Muriel Cantor, *op. cit.*

[24] Sandra Bem and Daryl Bem, "Does Sex Biased Job Advertising 'Aid and Abet' Sex Discrimination?" *Journal of Applied Social Psychology,* 3 (1973), pp. 6–18.

[25] For a review, see S. Pingree and R. Hawkins, "Children and Media," in Butler and Paisley, *op. cit.*

[26] Suzanne Pingree, *op. cit.;* Robert Hawkins, "The Dimensional Structure of Children's Perceptions of Television Reality," *Communication Research,* in press.

[27] See, for example, Vernon Stone, "Attitudes Toward Television Newswomen," *Journal of Broadcasting,* 18 (1974), pp. 49–61; Dan Drew and Susan H. Miller, "Sex Stereotypes and Reporting" (Paper presented at the meetings of the Association for Education in Journalism, August, 1976).

[28] Gaye Tuchman, *op. cit.*

[29] Daniel Boorstin, "From News-Gathering to News-Making: A Flood of Pseudo-Events," in Wilbur Schramm and Donald F. Roberts, *op. cit.*

[30] J. W. Johnstone, E. J. Slawski and W. W. Bowman, "The Professional Values of American Newsmen," *Public Opinion Quarterly,* 36 (1973), pp. 522–40.

About the Contributors

Edie N. Goldenberg, Assistant Professor of Political Science, University of Michigan. Educated at M.I.T. (S.B.) and Stanford University (M.A., Ph.D.), Professor Goldenberg has been a AAAS Mass Media Internship Fellow, a Danforth Foundation Fellow, a Woodrow Wilson Fellow, Scholar-in-Residence on newspaper reporting problems, Aspen Institute for Humanistic Studies, and reporter for the *Boston Globe*. She is the author of *Making the Papers* and articles on the news media and political behavior. She is working currently on an analysis of Congressional candidate campaign expenditures in 1976, with particular emphasis on the relationship between media expenditure patterns and deviations from the normal vote.

Doris A. Graber, Professor of Political Science, University of Illinois, Chicago Circle. Professor Graber received her B.A. and M.A. from Washington University and her Ph.D. from Columbia University. She was the Social Science College editor for Harper & Row (1956–63), an editor of U.S. Supreme Court Digest and Legal Periodical Digest for Commerce Clearing House, and has had editorial and reportorial part-time jobs for a number of weekly and daily newspapers. She has lectured extensively in the United States, Europe, Africa, Australia and Latin America. She was President of the Midwest Political Science Association in 1972–73. Her latest book is *Verbal Behavior and Politics*. Her current research is in the development of measurement techniques for appraising content in the electronic and print media, and in developing new techniques for measuring mass media effects on individual opinion formation.

Robert Parker Hawkins, Assistant Professor, Mass Communication Research Center, School of Journalism and Mass Communication, University of Wisconsin—Madison. Professor Hawkins was educated at Michigan State University (B.A.) and at Stanford University (M.A., Ph.D.). He is the author of many articles and papers on the role of mass media in socialization, the development of communication skills, the child's construction of social reality and sex-role definitions and socialization.

Maxwell E. McCombs, John Ben Snow Professor of Newspaper Research, School of Public Communications, Syracuse University. Professor McCombs received his B.A. from Tulane University and his M.A. and Ph.D. from Stanford University. He has been a reporter for the New Orleans *Times-Picayune* and is currently Director of the ANPA News Research Center. He is the author of numerous articles, books, monographs and papers on media and politics.

Suzanne Pingree, Lecturer, Women's Studies Program, University of Wisconsin—Madison. Professor Pingree was educated at the University of California, Santa Barbara (B.A.), and Stanford University (M.A., Ph.D.). She has been a writer, editor and cartoonist for ERIC Clearinghouse on Teacher Education. She was the Co-Chair of the Committee on the Status of Women for the Association for Education in Journalism and for the International Communication Association. She is the author of articles and papers on mass media and socialization, communication process and effects, and children's attitudes and patterns of communication.

Patricia Rice, feature writer, St. Louis *Post-Dispatch*. Ms. Rice has worked for the *Post-Dispatch* since 1969. Prior to that she worked in Paris as a journalist. She was one of three women invited to a two-week European-American Conference on politics and defense sponsored by the British Foreign Service at Wilton Park, England, in September, 1975. She has worked on several projects for the Eagleton Center for Women in American Politics, Rutgers University, including a conference for 50 state female state legislators in 1972 and with the Campaign '76 study of women in ten states. She has interviewed most major women politicians in the United States, England and France. She is the author of a chapter in a book supported by the Carnegie Foundation on Women in Politics and is author of *The Eclectic Shopper*.

Gertrude Joch Robinson, Associate Professor of Sociology, McGill University. Professor Robinson was educated at Swarthmore (A.B.), University of Chicago (M.A.) and the University of Illinois (Ph.D.). She received the Yugoslav Government Grant for her doctoral research. She is the author of numerous articles and monographs on cross-national aspects of journalism.

Leon V. Sigal, Associate Professor of Government, Wesleyan University. Professor Sigal received his B.A. from Yale and his Ph.D. from Harvard. He has been a Legislative Intern, Office of U.S. Representative Morris K. Udall; a Management Intern, U.S. Bureau of the Budget; and an Adviser to the Vietnam Moratorium Committee National Staff, 1969. He was the Border States Director of the McCarthy for President national campaign staff. He has participated in numerous conferences on politics and the mass media; he authored *Reporters and Officials.*

MaryAnn Yodelis Smith, Associate Professor, School of Journalism and Mass Communication, University of Wisconsin—Madison. Educated at Briarcliff College (B.A.) and the University of Wisconsin (M.A., Ph.D.), Professor Smith was a writer and editor for the *Sioux City Journal* and the *Des Moines Register.* She received the University of Wisconsin—Madison Chancellor's Award for Distinguished Teaching in 1975. In 1974 and 1975 she was the recipient of the Society of Professional Journalists Faculty Recognition Award. She is a member of the Editorial Advisory Boards of *Journalism Quarterly, Journalism History* and *Journalism Monographs.* She is a former Chairperson of the Committee on the Status of Women in Journalism and Education and is active in the Association for Education in Journalism. She is the author of numerous articles on journalism.

About the Editor

Laurily Keir Epstein, Assistant Professor of Political Science, Rutgers College, Rutgers University. Educated at Washington University (A.B., M.A., Ph.D.), Professor Epstein was Assistant to the Chancellor at Washington University. She is the editor of *Women in the Professions* and is the author of articles on political participation and women in politics. Her current research includes projects on news definitions, state programs for the elderly, historical voting patterns, and social context theories of political behavior.

Index

139